INDIAN
SCOUT CRAFT
AND LORE

Photo. by F. W. Waugh.

PORTRAIT OF THE AUTHOR, DR. CHARLES A. EASTMAN
(*OHIYESA*).

INDIAN
SCOUT CRAFT
AND LORE

(FORMERLY TITLED: INDIAN SCOUT TALKS)

BY

CHARLES A. EASTMAN
("Ohiyesa")

DOVER PUBLICATIONS, INC.
NEW YORK

Published in Canada by General Publishing Company, Ltd., 30 Lesmill Road, Don Mills, Toronto, Ontario.

Published in the United Kingdom by Constable and Company, Ltd., 10 Orange Street, London WC 2.

This Dover edition, first published in 1974, is an unabridged and unaltered republication of the work originally published by Little, Brown and Company in 1914 under the title *Indian Scout Talks: A Guide for Boy Scouts and Camp Fire Girls.*

International Standard Book Number: 0-486-22995-5
Library of Congress Catalog Card Number: 73-90637

Manufactured in the United States of America
Dover Publications, Inc.
180 Varick Street
New York, N.Y. 10014

These chapters represent the actual experiences and first-hand knowledge of the author. His training was along these lines, until he was nearly sixteen years of age. It is with the earnest hope that they may prove useful to all who venture into the wilderness in pursuit of wisdom, health, and pleasure, that they are dedicated to

THE BOY SCOUTS OF AMERICA

AND

THE CAMP FIRE GIRLS OF AMERICA

ACKNOWLEDGMENT

The author acknowledges the courtesy of "Boys' Life," "The Boy's World," "The Churchman," "The Youth's Companion," and "St. Nicholas," in permitting the use of chapters of this book which first appeared in their pages.

CONTENTS

CHAPTER   PAGE

I. At Home with Nature 1

II. Indian Methods of Physical Training 7

III. How to Make Friends with Wild Animals 15

IV. The Language of Footprints . . . 25

V. Hunting with Sling-shot and Bow and Arrow 34

VI. Primitive Modes of Trapping and Fishing 42

VII. How to Make and Handle Indian Canoes 48

VIII. The Camp Site and the Carry . . 55

IX. How to Build Wigwams and Shelters . 61

X. Fire Without Matches and Cooking Without Pots 69

XI. How to Make and Follow a Blazed Trail 77

XII. Indian Signals in Camp and Field . 85

XIII. An Indian Boy's Sports 91

XIV. A Winter Masque 99

XV. An Indian Girl's Sports 106

XVI. Indian Names and Their Significance 112

XVII. Indian Girls' Names and Symbolic Decorations 120

CHAPTER		PAGE
XVIII.	THE LANGUAGE OF FEATHERS AND CEREMONIAL DRESS	126
XIX.	INDIAN CEREMONIES FOR BOY SCOUTS	137
XX.	THE MAIDENS' FEAST: A CEREMONY FOR GIRLS	146
XXI.	THE GESTURE-LANGUAGE OF THE INDIAN	151
XXII.	INDIAN PICTURE-WRITING	159
XXIII.	WOOD-CRAFT AND WEATHER WISDOM	168
XXIV.	THE ART OF STORY-TELLING	175
XXV.	ETIQUETTE OF THE WIGWAM	182
XXVI.	TRAINING FOR SERVICE	188

LIST OF ILLUSTRATIONS

PORTRAIT OF THE AUTHOR, DR. CHARLES A. EAST-
MAN . . . . *Frontispiece*

FIGURE | PAGE

1. METHOD OF TRACKING A MOOSE . . . 32
2. FRAMEWORK OF THE WIGWAM 62
3. THE WIGWAM 63
4. FRAMEWORK OF THE TEEPEE 65
5. THE TEEPEE 65
6. IMPLEMENTS FOR MAKING A FIRE WITHOUT
MATCHES 70
7. MAKING THE FIRE 71
8–10. GROUND ARROWS 94, 96
11. INDIAN SYMBOL FOR THE HOME . . . 120
12. INDIAN SYMBOL FOR THE FOUR POINTS OF THE
COMPASS 121
13. INDIAN SYMBOL FOR LIFE HERE AND HERE-
AFTER 121
14. INDIAN SYMBOL FOR HAPPINESS IN THE HOME 121
15. INDIAN SYMBOL FOR ETERNAL UNION . . 121
16. INDIAN SYMBOL FOR FOOTPRINTS . . . 121
17. INDIAN SYMBOL FOR LIGHTNING OR DE-
STRUCTION 122
18. INDIAN SYMBOL FOR MOUNTAINS OR PRAYER 122
19. FIGURE OF THE THUNDER - BIRD . . . 143
20. THE PEACE PIPE 145
21–26. INDIAN PICTURE WRITINGS . . . 160–166

INDIAN
SCOUT CRAFT
AND LORE

I

AT HOME WITH NATURE

TO be in harmony with nature, one must be true in thought, free in action, and clean in body, mind, and spirit. This is the solid granite foundation of character.

Have you ever wondered why most great men were born in humble homes and passed their early youth in the open country? There a boy is accustomed to see the sun rise and set every day; there rocks and trees are personal friends, and his geography is born with him, for he carries a map of the region in his head. In civilization there are many deaf ears and blind eyes. Because the average boy in the town has been deprived of close contact and intimacy with nature, what he has learned from books he soon forgets, or is unable to apply. All learning is a dead language to him who gets it at second hand.

It is necessary that you should live with nature, my boy friend, if only that you may verify to your own satisfaction your schoolroom lessons. Further than this, you may be able to correct some error, or even to learn something that will be a real contribution to the sum of human knowledge. That is by no means impossible to a sincere observer. In the great laboratory of nature there are endless secrets yet to be discovered.

We will follow the Indian method, for the American Indian is the only man I know who accepts natural things as lessons in themselves, direct from the Great Giver of life.

Yet there exists in us, as in you, a dread of strange things and strange places; light and darkness, storm and calm, affect our minds as they do yours, until we have

learned to familiarize ourselves with earth
and sky in their harsher aspects. Suppose
that you are absolutely alone in the great
woods at night! The Indian boy is taught
from babyhood not to fear such a situation,
for the laws of the wilderness must necessarily be right and just, and man is almost
universally respected by the animals, unless
he himself is the aggressor. This is the
normal attitude of trust in our surroundings, both animate and inanimate; and if
our own attitude is normal, the environment at once becomes so. It is true that
an innate sense of precaution makes us
fear what is strange; it is equally true that
simplicity and faith in the natural wins in
the end.

I will tell you how I was trained, as a
boy, to overcome the terror of darkness and
loneliness. My uncle, who was my first
teacher, was accustomed to send me out
from our night camp in search of water.
As we lived a roving life in pursuit of
game, my errand led me often into pathless

and unfamiliar woods.   While yet very young, all the manhood and self-reliance in me was called forth by this test.

You can imagine how I felt as I pushed forward alone into the blackness, conscious of real danger from possible wild beasts and lurking foes.   How thrilling, how tantalizing the cry of the screech-owl!   Even the rustling of a leaf or the snapping of a dry twig under foot sent a chill through my body.   Novice that I was, I did not at once realize that it is as easy as swimming;   all I needed was confidence in myself and in the elements.

As I hurried through the forest in the direction my uncle had indicated, there seemed gradually to develop sufficient light for me to distinguish the trees along my way.   The return trip was easier.   When, as often happened, he sent me for a second pailful, no protest or appeal escaped my lips, thanks to my previous training in silent obedience.   Instinct helped me, as he had foreseen, to follow the trail I had made, and the trees were already old acquaintances. I could hear my own breathing in the silence; my footfall and heartbeat sounded as though they were those of another person coming behind me, and while this disturbed me at first, I quickly became accustomed to it. Very soon I learned to distinguish different kinds of trees by the rustling of their leaves in the breeze which is caused by the stir of man or animal.

If you can accustom yourself to travel at night, how much more you will be able to see and appreciate in the daytime! You will become more sensible of the unseen presences all about you and understand better the communications of the wild creatures. Once you have thrown off the handicap of physical fear, there will develop a feeling of sympathetic warmth, unknown before.

In the event of sudden danger, I was taught to remain perfectly motionless — a dead pause for the body, while the mind acts quickly yet steadily, planning a means of escape. If I discover the enemy first, I may be passed undiscovered. This rule is followed by the animals as well. You will find it strictly observed by the young ones who are hidden by their mother before they are able to run with her; and they are made to close their eyes also. The shining pupil of the eye is a great giveaway.

It is wonderful how quickly and easily one can adjust himself to his surroundings in wild life. How gentle is the wild man when at peace! how quick and masterful in action! Like him, we must keep nature's laws, develop a sound, wholesome body, and maintain an alert and critical mind. Upon this basis, let us follow the trail of the Indian in his search for an earthly paradise!

II

INDIAN METHODS OF PHYSICAL TRAINING

THE desire to be a man — the native spirit of the explorer and the hero — this is the strong inner motive which leads a boy out on the wilderness trail to discover the world anew. First of all, he discovers what he himself must be in order to overcome difficulties, to resist pain and hardship, and to win the object of his quest.

With these impulses at their purest and strongest, the Indian boy begins his career with the building of a sound and efficient body. The rivers and lakes present themselves as obstacles in his path, and as a very young child he starts in to swim, as naturally, almost, as he begins to walk. The writer barely remembers standing on the

white, pebbly beach with his grandfather
at his side; standing silent, full of sincere
reverence for the spirit of the deep, as he
stood before the towering cliff, or the ma-
jestic, solitary tree. In advance of every
undertaking, the Indian loves to meet thus
the all-pervading Spirit in the attitude of
wordless prayer.

Now the grandfather makes the plunge
with a boyish shout. " See, see! " he calls
to the boy as he comes up, breathless and
exultant, from his dive. " I am happy as
I lie here cradled by the yielding water.
You can be as happy, if you will but make
up your mind to try! "

Do you see the idea? The simple effort,
the plunge, that is the important thing.
The boy is neither frightened nor forced;
he follows soon of his own accord, and the
lesson is begun aright under the eye of an
experienced master.

As the child grows, he becomes more and
more expert and daring; from this time on
he eagerly seeks perfection in his new art.

His idea of perfection is, first, endurance, then swiftness; grace and form come naturally while aiming at these two. Therefore he swims at all times, in rough water and against strong currents. When some day he is cast suddenly into the water at a disadvantage, wounded, it may be, or obliged to swim long under water in order to escape the enemy, he knows how to utilize his strength to the utmost, and often overcomes tremendous odds with the remarkable tact and skill of the Indian athlete.

Clear your mind of all dread and suspicion; this is the first step in the wilderness life. Think not the water will drown you, or that anything in the water or on land will bite or poison you. Have confidence in nature and yourself. Perhaps three-fourths of your physical failures are due to lack of nerve and will-power.

It is not my purpose to teach you to swim, but to tell you how to use the art of swimming toward perfecting an out-of-door body and a logical mind. The Indian

swims freely at all seasons of the year when
the water is open. The usual method of
bathing in winter is to go into a sweat
lodge (the original Turkish bath) for five
or more minutes; then he jumps into a hole
in the ice, which he has cut large enough
to enter safely, and comes out in a few
minutes. After a short run, he wraps himself in a buffalo robe with the hair inside
and sleeps for a while. This makes him a
new man. The Indian boy often rolls in
the snow naked when fresh snow is on the
ground.

A perfectly trained outdoor man has
much natural heat in his body, and can
generate much more by exercise. Little
clothing is actually needed, and I have seen
Indians sleep all night without covering,
in fairly cool weather at that. Much depends upon habit and early training; yet
it is quite possible to learn new habits after
one is well grown.

One of the first things to do is to accustom yourself to lie on the ground until

your muscles make the necessary adjust-
ment to its hardness and unevenness, and
you can rest in comfort. Do not worry
about snakes or insects; they will rarely
do you harm; nor is there any danger from
dampness, once you are in training. A few
evergreen boughs over frozen or wet ground
are protection enough. The best way to
sleep in camp is feet toward the fire. There
are several reasons for this. If, by any
mischance, the fire escapes, your feet are
very sensitive and will awaken you in time.
Also, it is easy to get up without disturbing
any one.

The Indian must always arouse every
fiber of his body before he begins the day.
The first thing he does when he awakes
is to stretch every limb to the utmost, and
finally the entire body. He takes pleasure
in the most tremendous yawns. He rises
and starts up the fire; then he runs to the
nearest stream or lake shore and either
plunges in or splashes the fresh cold water
upon his face, chest, and arms. Often he

holds his face and eyes under water for several seconds. After that, he rinses his mouth and throat, rubs himself vigorously with the palms of his hands, and combs his hair, with the placid pool or spring for his only mirror.

In awakening his sleeping body, the Indian patterns after his animal friends. You will observe that no dog gets up and walks off without thoroughly stretching himself, from the nose to the tip of his tail. This is an excellent cure for early morning laziness.

Before winter sets in, he begins to take ice-cold foot-baths, and as soon as the first snow comes, he walks barefoot in it until he gets up a fine glow; then puts on warm, fur-lined moccasins. He is perfectly able to enjoy life out-of-doors at any season of the year, and has no use for the artificial house-heat of civilization. If he wets his feet at any time, he puts dry hair or even grass inside his moccasins, and runs until his feet are dry and warm.

The Indian's stomach is very strong, and this is something you should look well to, for much depends upon a perfect digestion. The teeth are valuable assistants, and these he exercises vigorously on tough muscle and fiber and keeps them clean without a toothbrush; in return they give him excellent service. He washes out his stomach twice a year, after fasting for twenty-four hours, by taking a mild decoction of herbs in a quart or two of lukewarm water and then tickling his throat with a feather. Sometimes he repeats the process.

His best meal is in the evening, when he eats heartily, sometimes taking another meal later in the night. His breakfast is a light one, and if he expects to run much, he eats nothing at all. At noon, he cooks some game for himself, if convenient. An occasional short fast is enjoined upon the Indian boy, as a means of developing his endurance and self-restraint.

Although trained from babyhood to

awaken easily, his sleep is sound and
sweet; such sleep as comes after a day of
healthful bodily exercise in the open air,
when a good evening meal and the warmth
of a cheerful camp-fire bring on that delicious drowsiness to which it is a luxury
to yield.

III

HOW TO MAKE FRIENDS WITH WILD ANIMALS

THERE is in the human mind a deep-seated and not wholly reasonable suspicion of the " silent people," as the Indian calls the wild animals, more especially of the hunting or carnivorous animals. They, on their part, are equally cautious, and take note of the scent as well as the looks and actions of the people they meet. Instinct is to them a sure guide, and when they do venture to disobey her voice, they almost always come to grief. Like children, the animals are very curious, and, even though terrified, they will sometimes stop to investigate the cause of their fright.

I have seen, in the old buffalo days upon the upper Missouri, a coyote or gray wolf go unnoticed by a herd of buffalo, elk, or even the timid antelope. The reason for this is that it was not the wolf's hunting season, which is when there are calves or fawns with the herd. Should a wolf come in sight at this time, every mother runs with her young for safety, and the whole herd becomes excited.

The wolf on the open prairie and the silver-tip bear, a near cousin to the grizzly, will sometimes take a fancy to keep company with you for several miles, if he thinks you did not see him. In such a case, he will not follow you, but keeps abreast, just far enough away to avoid discovery. He will occasionally stop and watch you from behind cover; but do not be alarmed! He has no intention of attacking you. Probably he has a home and little ones not far off, and wishes to assure himself that the stranger has no designs upon his peace.

It is well known to Indian hunters that no animal offers battle to man except under very strong provocation. The grizzly bear is the notable exception to this rule. Others, even the so-called ferocious beasts, need not be feared except when pushed to the wall.

No doubt you have been more or less influenced by what you have read in books of adventure, which are mainly highly spiced fiction. If I were to relate to you all the fireside stories of the wild Indian, whose hunters were constantly in the field, you would find that hand-to-hand combats with beasts were few indeed. If the buffalo and other large animals were aggressive in temper, what chance had the poor Indian — on foot, and, before the coming of the European, armed only with bow and arrows or a bone spear?

There are several things, therefore, which you may put down as general truths. First, the animals are accustomed to mind strictly their own business and are not likely to interfere with you unless you molest them first. Second, there is a way to learn the peculiarity of each and make his acquaintance. Third, it is possible to influence them greatly, even in critical circumstances, by firmness and self-control.

If ever a grizzly bear happens to charge upon you, with wide-open lips showing his powerful teeth and eyes flashing with anger, have the nerve to stand your ground! Without moving a muscle, your eyes fixed on his, you may threaten him with a mere sharp stick, and he will change his mind. He growls, but you do not answer his challenge; he concludes to pass on. Here is a clear demonstration of our Indian axiom: " Silence is greater than speech."

A few years ago, an instance of this kind came to my ears among the Assiniboine Sioux. Four Stars, a brave, followed one side of a deep gulch while his two companions were on the other side, hunting deer. As he approached the ravine, which was full of wild cherry and plum bushes, his friends saw from the opposite bank a female silver-tip with her two nearly full-grown cubs lurking within the thicket. They made every effort to attract his attention, but in vain. He walked right down the slope, apparently to his death.

When the three bears charged, Four Stars was taken completely by surprise, but he showed no fear. He stopped short in his tracks and assumed a rigid pose, his old single-loading musket extended from his shoulder. The bears came on until they could plainly see his eyes; then they paused and crouched, displaying their teeth and claws. A puff of smoke from Four Stars' gun; the mother fell and rolled on the ground. The young bears leaped savagely forward, but the young man ripped off his shirt and threw it in their path, causing them to hesitate. Meanwhile, as his ejector was broken, he used a ramrod to push out the shell of his cartridge, calmly re-loaded and fired, killing the two.

Here was a hero. The odds were against him. He knew the peculiar weakness of the foe, but to take advantage of this knowledge required something equally important — the nerve of a master man!

I need scarcely tell you that the animals are suspicious of man. They have every reason to be. You must have real love and sympathy for them and be consistent and straightforward in your dealings, in order to gain their friendship. They will accept your peace-offering of food as soon as they trust you, and in many cases their confidence is not hard to win.

Some will come to you when called, and a very interesting instance of this occurred last summer, at the country home of a friend upon the Rock River in Illinois. While a group of us sat on the veranda, I gave an imitation of the mother rabbit's whistle; and, to our delighted surprise, a tiny rabbit crept out from under the big leaves of some plants near the house. It came trustingly up close to the railing, and sat there watching us out of its bright eyes until I gave the cry of the coyote, when the little thing raced for cover!

The mother's call and the mating or lover's call of different animals may be successfully imitated with practice and with or without the use of a birch-bark horn or other adjunct. A good imitation is always answered if in season, and if the animal called is within hearing.

On the prairies and the great lakes you can attract animals to you by means of signals. This method is based entirely upon their insatiable desire to investigate whatever is strange to them. You may tie something red to a long stick and set it upright in full view of antelopes, yourself lying motionless near by, and they will come very close to inspect it. The sand-hill crane will do the same; and if you flap your hat or the corner of a blanket while lying flat, the Canadian geese will circle about you and sometimes alight.

But the great secret of establishing intercourse with wild animals is to rove in their domain without doing them harm. In this way they come to know you long before you have made their acquaintance. I cannot tell you how they know when to trust you, but know they do!

If you are near a lake where water-fowl congregate, take your canoe at evening or in the early morning and paddle quietly here and there for several days, and I will guarantee that you will be a privileged character upon that lake. They will mind you no more than they would mind a musk-rat, and you will have a splendid opportunity to study the character and ways of each species.

As to an individual or personal friendship with a wild creature, the best way is to bring one up from infancy, yet allow it perfect freedom. In this the Indian succeeded remarkably well; and it was not uncommon for him to establish an intimacy with an adult animal or bird, although this is a more difficult feat. You must bear in mind that knowing a captive or domestic animal is not at all the same thing, as their habits and manners are strongly influenced by an artificial environment.

One morning my friend Simon Bonga, a three-quarters blood Ojibway at Leech Lake in Minnesota, found a baby fawn not more than thirty yards from his house. He took some milk to it and left it there. The next day he took some more, and soon the fawn would drink from his hand. After a few days, he would simply stand in his doorway and give the mother call. The fawn would run to him to be fed. A little later, not only he but his wife and children were able to stroke and pet the little one, which continued to live in its native haunts, but came regularly to the house for food and a frolic. The mother was seen once or twice, but made no trouble.

A year later, I wrote to Mr. Bonga and incidentally referred to the fawn. He replied: " She is now a respectable young lady doe, and we are much attached to her." She has lived the natural life and has yet allowed herself the advantage of intimate association with human beings, while my friend and his family have known the charm of close familiarity with one of nature's most graceful creations.

IV

THE LANGUAGE OF FOOTPRINTS

YOU have often heard it said that " actions speak louder than words." It is a fact that both voluntary and involuntary actions of the body tell truly the mind's purpose, and this is why the Indian studies so assiduously every record of the comings and goings of his fellow creatures, both animal and human.

The footprint, I want you to bear in mind, is first of all a picture of all the prominent points on the sole. The ball of the foot, the heel and toes, hoof and claw, each makes its own impress. Even the fishes make theirs with their fins, which to them are hand and foot. This is the wood-dweller's autograph. More than this, each series of footprints tells a bit of history, perhaps betrays a secret to the instructed eye, and the natural Indian did not neglect to drill his child thoroughly in this important branch of learning.

I will now ask you to enter the forest with me. First, scan the horizon and look deep into the blue vault above you, to adjust your nerves and the muscles of your eye, just as you do other muscles by stretching them. There is still another point. You have spread a blank upon the retina, and you have cleared the decks of your mind, your soul, for action.

Let us divide our scouts into small groups; one alone is sometimes best, when you are pretty well advanced in this study, but at first two or three, with a head scout or teacher, will do. We will assume that you have passed the primary test; that is, you have learned to recognize the footprints of mice, birds, squirrels, rabbits, and perhaps to some extent the next set, those of the dog, the cat, the fox, and the wolf.

It is a crisp winter morning, and upon the glistening fresh snow we see everywhere the story of the early hours — now clear and plain, now tangled and illegible — where every traveler has left his mark upon the clean, white surface for you to decipher.

The first question is: Who is he? The second: Where is he now? Around these two points you must proceed to construct your story.

If the snow is not deep, the imprint of the toes and even the claw marks are very distinct, but in deep, soft snow you have only the holes made by the foot and leg. Some animals, such as the cow, drag their feet, while the wolf kind make a mark much like the print of a cane. This is also true of the cat family. The distinguishing difference is in the gait, as shown in the relative position of the footprints, and this is a matter that calls for careful attention. The break in each print is usually greater behind than before, and this tells you in which direction the animal is going.

The rabbit makes innumerable tracks as soon as it stops snowing, and we may be sure that its burrow is not far distant, for unless food is scarce or danger imminent, they will not leave their own immediate locality. As to larger animals, love-affairs often lead them far afield, and wolves and bears cover much ground; yet even they have their favorite haunts, and they are masters of their map. All these things the student of footprints should bear in mind.

It is essential to estimate as closely as you can how much of a journey you will undertake if you determine to follow a particular trail. Many factors enter into this. When you come upon the trail, you must if possible ascertain when it was made. Examine the outline; if that is undisturbed, and the loose snow left on the surface has not yet settled, the track is very fresh, as even an inexperienced eye can tell. Next determine the sex, and finally the age, if you can: all these enter into the problem of getting your game. It is easy to tell the sex of the deer family by their footprints; the female has sharper hoofs and a narrower foot, while the male has rounded points to the hoofs.

It will also be necessary to consider the time of year. It is of no use to follow a buck when he starts out on his travels in the autumn, and with the moose or elk it is the same. If the track is a running one, the question is: Was it in play or in flight? Look at the toes; if they are widely spread, he was running for sport and exercise; if close together, it was a race for life.

Many animals for safety's sake go through a series of manœuvers before they lie down to rest. For instance, at the end of the trail they make two loops, and conceal themselves at a point where the pursuer must, if he sticks to the trail, pass close by their hiding-place and give timely warning of his approach. This trick is characteristic of the deer and rabbit families.

The tracking of an animal in summer is naturally much more difficult than in winter, unless the footprints are on soft ground. The Indian hunter is then even keener in his observations; he looks for the displacement of leaves and blades of grass, or for broken dry sticks. These slight displacements will adjust themselves in a short time, to be sure; but in hunting, the fresh track is what is wanted. Other tracks are not much followed, except those of man or bear from whom danger is to be feared. A new trail, especially one made during a dewy night, is easy to trace the next morning, and on the open prairie the reflection of sun on the grass blades helps, so that sometimes a few paces away one may see the trail clearly.

Referring to winter trailing, I remember well an example of perfect accuracy set by my uncle, who was a famous hunter. I was then a boy of about fifteen, living in

the wilds of Manitoba. We came suddenly
upon a moose track, evidently made on
the day before, as the upturned snow was
frosted over by a night's cold. He stopped
and surveyed the lay of the country. A
little way ahead a ravine led down to a
lake, of which the outlet was densely
wooded with willows and birches. We
followed the trail down the ravine and
along the lake shore until we reached this
stream, and here my uncle paused and
climbed a tree. When he came down, he
examined his gun and put in a fresh load,
then proceeded cautiously a few paces,
when we came upon another trail crossing
the first almost at right angles. It, too,
was a day old. To my surprise, my uncle
now motioned to me to stay where I was,
and throwing off some of his garments
and adjusting his moccasins, he ran back
on his trail. I waited about half an hour,
when I heard the report of his gun, and
soon after he returned with the good news:
" I got him! "

The diagram shows you how it was done. The moose had covered his position by a swinging loop, and was lying down facing the first turn. At that time of year they may remain thus for several days. He had seen that we did not enter the loop and felt safe. My uncle, knowing the

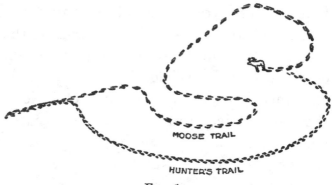

MOOSE TRAIL

HUNTER'S TRAIL

FIG. 1.

trick, had run back a hundred yards or so, then circled behind the loop, and approached him from the rear, where he easily brought him down.

Among the Indians, the study of human footprints was carried to a fine point. Many of us would be able to say at a glance, Here goes So-and-So, with perfect accuracy. Even the children would recognize instantly the footprint of a stranger from another tribe. It was claimed by some that character may be read from the footprint, just as some white people undertake to read it from the handwriting, on the ground that certain characteristic attitudes and motions of the body, reflecting mental peculiarities, affect the gait and consequently the pedal autographs. At any rate, our people are close readers of character, and I do not hesitate to say that faithful study of the language of footprints in all its details will be certain to develop your insight as well as your powers of observation.

V

HUNTING WITH SLING - SHOT AND BOW AND ARROW

IT is likely that the earliest weapon of primitive man was that employed by the shepherd David, — the little round pebble from the brook. It was not despised as a last resort by the Indians of my day, and we boys practised with it continually.

It was customary with us to carry about a dozen or so small rounded stones in a special leather pouch. We used soft buckskin thongs about eighteen inches long, attached to a piece of flexible rawhide some two inches square, but usually tapered to a point, for the sling. This was our long distance gun; but the first step toward learning its use is the throwing of stones accurately by hand.

I remember when I was about ten years old that my favorite playmate, Redhorn, and I used to spend many long mornings perfecting ourselves in this art, and we kept up our practice until we could hit the animal or object aimed at as many times as you boys would with a 22 or an air gun.

This training of the eye together with the muscles of the arm is the first essential. The next is to throw with all your strength and still keep your aim true. After mastering the overhand throw, we practised several other varieties, including one straight up in the air, which helps in the development of waist and back muscles.

We boys hunted squirrels, rabbits, partridges, and ducks with stones merely, and often succeeded as well as if we had had arrows or even guns. One advantage of this method is that it is silent and scarcely disturbs the game. It is especially lively in the fall of the year, when game is abundant and often young and inexperienced.

At this time we often hunted in groups.
In case of a party of six boys, four would
take up positions on a point of the lake
shore, while the other two swam out into
the lake, making as much noise as possible
and imitating the screams of the hawk or
eagle to frighten the ducks. Sometimes
hundreds would rise with a thunder of
wings and fly over our heads in large flocks.
Then our innocent-looking pebbles whis-
tled through the air like real bullets, and
at every volley several ducks would drop
into the water for the swimmers to pick
up, while flock followed flock in quick
succession. At such times we were happy
and gave many a warwhoop and yell of
delight; though it is true the swimmers
were in some danger from stray shots, and
had often to dive to escape the missiles.

If the ducks are wild, they may be de-
ceived by stripping off your clothing, daub-
ing your body with mud, and lying motionless on the shore. When we had killed
enough, we had the excitement of chasing

the wounded ducks in the water, and at last we counted our bag and divided equally. No boy who is not a good shot should hunt in a group with others, as there is danger of injuring his companions.

Upon the western prairies there are in some places small alkali lakes, where few or no stones are to be found. Here we used the sticky alkali mud, on the end of a pliable rod or willow switch perhaps two and a half feet long. The lump is about the size of a hen's egg and the consistency of artist's clay. It is thrown with one swing of the arm, and as a rule only stuns the duck, so that it is necessary to pick up your game after each volley, otherwise it may come to life and fly away. In an emergency, when no willows were to be had, the Indian boy sometimes used his arrow, first removing the head and the feathers.

The Indian uses a shorter bow than do most primitive people. The regulation hunting-bow is less than five feet long,

and some of the most convenient ones are
only four feet. The best bows are made
of young elm, oak, hickory, ash, and dog-
wood. Ironwood is good, but not commonly found. There are also elk horn
and Rocky Mountain sheep horn bows,
as well as buffalo rib bows, which are
worked to perfect shape by the use of
steam. They are usually made in two
pieces, are difficult to make, and highly
valued. The boy's ordinary bow is made
of any kind of wood, but always that from
a sapling, so as to get the necessary elasticity.

The continuous curve bow is not ap-
proved by us, as one made with concave
ends and convex in the middle is easier to
control and does not jerk the arrow off its
true direction. As soon as the Indian has
shaped it by whittling, he dries it in proper
form, and oils it while seasoning to keep
it supple. When thoroughly seasoned, he
finishes it by scraping and rubbing with
the natural sandstone. He then tightly

winds each end and the middle with flat sinew and notches the ends for the bow-string, which is best made of sinew, though wild hemp and other materials are used on occasion.

In all my wild life, I never saw arrows made of split wood. The young choke-cherry and June-berry furnish most of the arrows, though the coast tribes some-times use reeds. The usual length is twenty-eight inches, including the head. They are about one-fourth of an inch in diameter and very light. The man's arrow is feath-ered with three feathers five inches long, but most boys' arrows have but two feathers, and these may be anywhere from two to five inches long, and must curve around the body of the arrow in screw fashion, otherwise it will not fly straight.

The Indians made arrow-heads of bone, horn, claws and bills of birds, and some-times of clam-shells. After the coming of the white man, they used iron. The stone arrow-head was used apparently by an earlier race, for most of those that we pick up are too heavy for the Indian arrow. As children, we often played with them but never made practical use of them, unless for shooting fish. Indeed, the boy's arrow needs no separate head, but is merely sharpened at the point, or has a knob at the end, in which case it needs no feather. This is the safest and most convenient weapon for shooting in the woods, for it brings down all small birds and animals, and is readily recovered.

When you have made your own bow and arrows, which you can easily do, the first thing to learn is the correct position for archery. Your attitude is that of one who is ready to jump from a springboard. Then you must accustom yourself to the strength and spring of your bow, and it is well to know your arrows individually, their swiftness and peculiarities of flight. The highest success in marksmanship depends partly upon one's natural gifts, yet faithful practice must bring a good degree of satisfaction. The arrow does not alarm the game, is not dangerous to the hunter or his companions, and seems to be distinctly the boy's weapon.

The exceptional Indian, with his sinew-backed, four-foot bow and bone-tipped arrow, was able to shoot clear through the body of a large animal, such as elk or buffalo, unless he chanced to hit bone. All Indians could kill the largest animal with this convenient weapon, using the quick off-hand shot. You can learn it, too.

VI

PRIMITIVE MODES OF TRAPPING AND FISHING

IT is boy's instinct to try to outwit and capture wild animals. This is as true of the outdoor boy among the whites as of the Indian boy. The point of interest in the Indian boy's way is that he depends more upon his own ingenuity and resources. While he is trying his grandfather's tricks, he often devises a better one.

The first trapping that I ever did was mere childish play, engaged in by Indian boys of seven to ten years old. We snared wild mice by placing slip-nooses of horsehair or fine sinew across their well-beaten thoroughfares. However, it is no easy thing to handle a mouse thus caught, for he can and will fight with his sharp teeth.

We used to turn them loose upon some islet or in a mimic fort of clay or sand, to watch and play with.

We also used the slip-knot for birds, especially crows and magpies, which may be attracted to the snares by a bait of fresh meat or corn. A few crows may be caught and hung up to drive their mates from the maize fields; or, by tying your solitary crow prisoner in a lonely place, he will summon all the rest to a pow-wow. This gives the boy, hidden near at hand, a fine opportunity to study their ways.

We caught squirrels with our bowstrings, on the same principle as the horsehair noose, only in this case we stayed by the trap, and when the squirrel put his head through, we pulled on the string. This works well with ground squirrels, or gophers, and prairie dogs, although in the case of the latter we sometimes caught one of his house-mates, the screech-owl or rattle-snake, instead.

The trapping of rabbits is a simple affair.

A bended sapling is secured above a rabbit run in such a manner that when the victim runs his head in the noose, he is swung high in the air. Partridges are caught in the same fashion.

A novel device for catching rabbits, in time of scarcity an important source of food supply, is to scatter large, sharp burrs along their runs. The burrs stick fast to their feet, they sit on their haunches to try to get them off, and so fall an easy prey to the boy hunters.

Perhaps you would like to try the log deadfall. To make this effective trap, you need a good knife or a hatchet — nothing more. First drive into the ground four stakes about the size of a broom-handle, one pair on either side of a rabbit furrow, if this is the game you are after. Leave just enough room between each pair for a good-sized log, which you may lay directly across the path. The stakes serve as gate-posts to your trap, and on either side you build a slight barricade of brush. Next take two round pegs and cut off the ends squarely at about three inches long, or longer, according to your game; smooth a place for them at either end of the log between the stakes, and upon them balance a second log, which is partly supported by the two pairs of stakes as well. The aperture, just big enough for a rabbit to squeeze through, is crossed by several hairs from a horse's tail tied to the supporting pins. The unsuspecting victim springs along, knocks out the underpinning, and the log falls upon him.

For larger game, such as the fox, mink, or fisher, two more logs are used, one end of each resting upon the upper log and the free end on the ground. This gives extra weight to the trap, which may be baited with a piece of meat, firmly attached to a string in such a way that when the animal tugs at the bait, the pins are pulled out and the trap falls. Indian men use this deadfall more than the boys.

Our fishing was even more primitive, since we were not provided with hook and line. Sometimes we would select a convenient water-hole and just below it build a rough dam of sticks and stones in a V shape, with the nose pointing down-stream. In the center of the dam we left a small opening, and just under it hung a cage or basket roughly woven of willows, projecting slightly above the surface of the water. It was great sport to wade the brook from a point some distance above the dam, poking under the banks with long sticks and slapping the water with flat paddles, so as to frighten the fish and drive them into our trap. When the basket was well filled, we shut off the opening in the dam with logs or stones, and proceeded to catch the fish with our bare hands, snare, or spear them.

If we did not care to go to the trouble of constructing a basket, we simply drove the fish into a deep hole with a rude dam below to prevent their escape, and caught

them by one of the methods named, or
by shooting with bow and arrow. But
we were never allowed to take more than
we really needed. If a surplus were caught,
we usually freed them, or stored them in
a small pond or spring where we could
study and play with them at our leisure.

The best time for taking large quantities
of fish, which may be dried or smoked for
future use, is in spawning time in early
spring, when most fishes migrate into
shallow water and are so sluggish that
they may be knocked on the head with
a club. At this season all kinds of wild
hunters, crows, wolves, wildcats, minks,
otters, come to the outlets of the lakes or
the banks of the streams for food, and my
people were not much behind them in this.
The streams of my boyhood days were
sometimes packed like a sardine can, and
we boys have more than once opened a
way and saved large numbers of fish from
suffocation.

VII

HOW TO MAKE AND HANDLE INDIAN CANOES

THERE are several different kinds of canoes made by Indians, of which the birch-bark canoe is the most generally available. The skin boats of the Esquimaux are larger and are skilfully made, but we are considering here only the handiwork of our own Indians.

The Plains Indians formerly used the buffalo-skin boat, called " bull-boat," but this is at best an emergency vessel, constructed only when they were forced to cross a river too deep to ford and too wide to swim. It can scarcely be called a boat and might be termed a raft of skins, for it cannot be paddled like the true canoe. It is probably the crudest form of native craft.

The bull-boat is made upon a framework of willow withes roughly woven into an oblong shape, using long poles for the bottom to give the necessary firmness. Over this frame rawhides are stretched, and sewed with sinew. The seams are smeared with tallow or gum. Two or three long strings are attached to the front end. Having loaded the unwieldy vessel to its full capacity with household goods and children, one or two persons would stand in it with long poles to shove, while two or three others swam ahead, pulling it by the ropes, and sometimes others pushed from behind. The bull-boat was easily capsized, therefore every precaution was taken against accident to the precious cargo. As soon as the stream was crossed, it was taken apart, and the materials put to other uses.

The dugout is much used where birch-bark is not obtainable. The tree, preferably basswood, cottonwood, or soft maple, is selected with care, the trunk cut the proper length, twelve to sixteen feet, roughly shaped externally, and then hollowed out with much pains. Some of these boats are very serviceable, and many Indians think them swifter as well as more durable than the birch canoe; but it is not safe for a novice to undertake to handle one. It is very graceful in the hands of an expert Indian canoeist, but in some respects still retains the characteristics of a log in water.

After the introduction of modern tools, the dugout became common throughout the Indian country, while the forest Indian alone still clung to the bark canoe. The white trapper, hunter, and explorer readily adopted the convenient dugout, but it has almost disappeared with these avocations; yet the boy hunter or camper who has the requisite patience can easily make his own.

The Indian makes his dugout by first hewing it roughly into the shape of a boat, then making crosswise cuts inside of the trunk about a foot apart and splitting the wood lengthwise between these cuts until well hollowed out. After this he uses a small pickaxe to cut still deeper, until the walls are from four to six inches in thickness; finally he smooths the surface with a chisel. On the outside the final work is done with the draw-knife or ordinary knife. Bone knives and sharp clam-shells were used in primitive times. Fire may be used to dry and polish.

Our Indian leaves his canoe to season sufficiently after making and before he launches it. He oils it instead of painting, as he has no paint. His paddles are shaped from any kind of light wood; always two in number, in order that he may have an extra one on hand.

The bark canoe requires more skill and labor to make, and is much more ornamental. In the first place, you need just the right kind of bark, and for this you must search through the woods. You must unbark many trees to obtain sheets of uniform thickness and elasticity, sound, and of the proper length and width. You will then temper and season them by laying them smoothly on the ground atop of one another, for some days or even weeks, every alternate one cross-grained, and weighted with stones or logs. Some bark is brittle and cracks easily, and this must be discarded. In early spring when the sap runs is the best time to gather bark.

The next thing is to secure the materials for your framework. The wood used is the swamp or white cedar. The Indian cuts down slender, limbless ones and splits them into convenient lengths, then whittles them flat, like boards, about two to four inches wide, and seasons them before they are fully finished. The longest are used for bracing the canoe lengthwise, usually four to six on the bottom and two to three on each side, beside the rim. The shorter ones are laid crosswise for the ribs, a foot or more apart, tapering to either

end. The crosspieces are four in number.
The Indian does not use these for seats,
but sits in the bottom of the canoe. His
canoe is from twelve to sixteen feet long,
and somewhat wider than the one the
white man makes.

After collecting and preparing your material, drive stakes into the ground a foot
apart in the exact shape of a canoe, and
within this arrange your ribs and braces
in the proper order, and tie them firmly
together with the long, pliable roots of
the swamp cedar or fir-tree. Sometimes
strips of the inner layer of basswood bark
are used for this purpose. When the frame
of the canoe is complete, remove it, and
lay the pieces of birch-bark, cut to the
pattern and partially sewed together, within
the pegged-out space. Allow a little for
seams and fitting. Now lay the frame
upon the covering, turn the latter up and
fit it smoothly, as a dress is fitted to the
manikin. An awl is used for making holes,
and the dried cedar roots for sewing the

bark. Turn the upper edges inward over the rim and sew them closely over and over. Lastly, take out, invert, and caulk all the seams well with boiling pitch outside, and inside with sturgeon blubber or glue made by boiling horn or rawhide.

Now your canoe is finished except for the decoration, which may consist of figures drawn with the awl on the soft bark, or of paintings on bow and stern. The conventionalized figure of some water-fowl or fish, such as the swan, loon, or sturgeon, forms an appropriate emblem, and may also serve to name your craft.

VIII

THE Indian exercises much ingenuity in selecting a suitable camp site. The first essentials are water and fuel; next comes sanitation and drainage, protection from the elements and from ready discovery by possible foes; finally, beauty of situation.

In midsummer, when Indians camp together in great numbers, they invariably choose an extensive plateau, either on the secondary bank of a river or lake, or upon the level bottom lands of some large stream. At this time of the year the ground is dry, and there is no danger from floods. For the winter camp, they prefer a protected site in deep woods, near a large river or lake.

In the case of a small party or a solitary traveler, concealment is the first principle to be observed.   Seclusion gives a sense of security, but one does not need to sacrifice to it his æsthetic sense.   The Indian is adept in selecting a most beautiful spot which commands all approaches, or a hidden cove, guarded by curving shores, but very near a long-distance view which he keeps for his look-out.

In the heat of the summer he often pitches his teepee upon a high, rocky point, to get away from the mosquitoes, but takes care that he is protected by other heights in such a way that any one approaching must come very near before he discovers the camp.   There are usually concealed approaches at the back and sides that afford a retreat in case of danger, and also serve as short cuts on his return from hunting or trapping.

In his forest life, it is a matter of course with him to leave the teepee poles just as they stand, removing only the covering.

This is not only a matter of convenience, but it may cause the enemy to delay and manœuver when they first sight the camp, thus giving him more time to retreat. Often the war-party discovers its mistake only after its intended victims have been gone for some hours. In case of a hasty retreat, the tent is left standing undisturbed and the log fire burning within, so that the smoke may be maintained as long as possible after the departure of the inmates. This was a convenient ruse in the old days.

It is best in camping to build small fires. This rule is observed by all Indians. Smoke may be seen at a great distance, especially on a clear day, and may be scented by the ordinary Indian a long way off, if the wind is right. Only in cold weather or for special purposes does the Indian indulge in a huge fire, and in no case does he ever leave it without seeing that it is entirely extinguished. If possible, he builds it upon the rocks, so that the ashes

may be removed by wind and rain, and
the ground show no disfigurement.

When a party camp together, the tents
are pitched in a circle. The entrance to
the circle is always toward the watering-
place, and the council lodge is placed opposite the entrance. If the party is a large
one, there may be more than one circle,
each band or clan having its own.

When a camp is to break up, it is decreed on the day before, the next camp
site having already been explored and
selected by men appointed for that purpose. One of these men may be named to
guide the caravan to the chosen spot.
The start is made before daybreak, and
the packing done most expeditiously and
in accordance with a well understood system, whether wagons, ponies, dogs, canoes, or men are used to transport belong-
ings from place to place. There is nothing
slovenly or haphazard about the Indian's
domestic economy, and packing is an interesting and important feature of camp-craft.

In the first place, if you are to transport your own equipment, you must use the carrying strap, which consists of two strings, each four to five feet long, attached strongly to each end of the flat chest and head pieces, which are about two inches wide and long enough to encircle the head and shoulders. The goods are secured in a well-balanced roll or bundle, and this bundle should not be carried too low. Place it to suit your strength and comfort, and do not let it sway or swing. It may be advisable to drop it and rest now and then, if the load is heavy or the distance considerable. The Indians can easily carry in this manner all that is required for an outing.

If you have packhorses, your goods must be made into bundles of convenient size and shape to balance one another on the two sides of the animal, and well secured with strong straps. Before the Indian obtained horses from the Spanish colonists, he traveled but a short day's journey, and carried with him only absolute necessities. All household effects had to be transported on the back, or by means of the dog travois. In fact, the travois was his primitive vehicle for many years after the advent of the horse. It consists merely of the tent poles and an oval basket, netted from strips of rawhide, which is also used as a door for the teepee. One pony can carry at most eight poles, four on a side. These are bound to the saddle, the tips forming an angle above the horse's head, and the free ends drag on the ground below the basket, which contains all the household goods, and sometimes young children.

IX

HOW TO BUILD WIGWAMS AND SHELTERS

THE Indian family almost always carry with them the necessary equipment for making camp, but hunters and solitary travelers must improvise something from the material at hand. The permanent village is composed of fairly substantial and rain-proof dwellings, called " teepees," " wigwams," and as many names as there are Indian languages. Slighter shelters are quickly put up in an emergency. You will enjoy copying some of these for your temporary or regular camp.

A substantial wigwam is built of poles and bark in either six-sided or octagonal form. In my day, we used six poles cut off at a fork about ten feet high. These are set two feet deep in the ground, eight to twelve feet apart, and joined by other  poles resting on the forked ends.   This forms the framework or hexagon.   There are four more poles in the center, forming a square, and also connected at the top, and in the middle of this little court a shallow hole is dug for a fireplace and lined with flat stones.

FIG. 2.

The outer wall of the bark house is of split poles driven into the ground quite close together and neatly overlaid with the bark of the birch, elm, or basswood, in strips eight feet long by four to six feet wide. The trees should be peeled if possible when the sap flows in spring, and the strips spread one upon another on the ground and weighted with stones, so as to dry smooth and flat. Between every two inner posts is an outside post to support the crosspieces, light saplings which hold the bark in position. You can also tie these crosspieces to the split poles with strips of tough cedar bark.

The roof is made in the same way of split poles covered with bark, the latter overlapping like shingles, so that it is water-proof. Over the fireplace is left an adjustable opening, to let out the smoke and let in light and air. The doorway is an opening in the middle of the south side, three feet by six, closed by a movable door of bark or raw- hide. A double row of posts with forked ends, about four feet

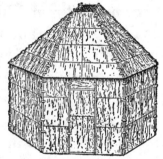

Fig. 3.

long and the same distance apart, are driven two feet deep into the ground around three sides of the shack on the inside, connected with lighter poles and crosspieces, then covered with smooth bark firmly tied in place. Here are spread robes

and blankets for beds by night and a loun-
ging-place by day. There should be sufficient space to move about between the
bunks and the fireplace.

This kind of shack may be thatched
with coarse meadow grass, instead of bark,
if it is more convenient to do so. Some
tribes make them partly underground for
warmth in winter, and when completely
covered with sods or earth the hexagon
becomes a " round house."

The greater number of Indians, however, built conical wigwams. If made of
the materials I have described, it was customary to transport the rolls of bark from
place to place; the poles were cut at each
new camp or left in place at the old ones.
Sometimes grass and rushes were braided
into mats and used as coverings and car-
pets. The Plains Indians used buffalo
hides, nicely tanned and sewed together
in semicircular shape.

The skeleton of the conical teepee is
made by tying three poles together near

the top, and, when raised, separating them
to form a tripod.   Against this place in a

FIG. 4.

circle as many poles as
you think necessary to
support your outer
covering of cloth or
thatch, usually twelve
to fifteen. If of canvas,
the covering is tied to
a pole and then raised
and wrapped about the framework and
secured with wooden pins to within about
three feet of the ground.

This space is left for
the entrance and
covered by a movable
door, which may be
merely a small blanket.
If you have nothing
better, a quantity of
dry grass will make you a warm bed.

FIG. 5.

Suppose an Indian brave starts out
alone, or with one companion, to lay in
a supply of meat or to trap for furs. All

the outfit he really needs is his knife and
hatchet, bow and arrows, with perhaps
a canoe, according to the country he has
to traverse. He proceeds on foot to a
good camping-place, and there builds his
shelter of whatever material is most abundant. If in the woods, he would probably
make it a " lean-to," which is constructed
thus:

In a dry and protected spot, find two
trees the right distance apart and connect
them by poles laid upon the forks of each
at a height of about eight feet. This forms
the support of your lean-to. Against this
horizontal bar place small poles close together, driving their ends in the ground,
and forming an angle with about the slant
of an ordinary roof. You can close in both
sides, or not, as you choose. If you leave
one open, build your fire opposite the
entrance, thus making a cheerful and airy
" open-face camp." Thatch from the
ground up with overlapping rows of flat
and thick evergreen boughs, and spread

several layers of the same for a springy
and fragrant bed. You can make a similar shelter of grass or rushes, but in this
case you must have the poles closer together.

The dome-shaped wigwam or "wicki-
up" is made in a few minutes almost anywhere by sticking into the ground in a
circle a sufficient number of limber poles,
such as willow wands, to make it the size
you need. Each pair of opposites is bent
forward until they meet, and the ends
interlocked and tied firmly. Use any convenient material for the covering; an
extra blanket will do.

You can make any of these tent shelters
with no tool save your hatchet or strong
knife. The object is to protect yourself
and your possessions from cold, wind,
rain, and the encroachment of animals.
As to the last, however, they are not likely
to trouble you unless very hungry, and
a fire is the best protection. He is the
natural and true man who utilizes every-

thing that comes in his way; a cave, a great hollow tree, even an overhanging rock serves for his temporary home, or he cheerfully spreads his bed under the starry night sky.

X

FIRE WITHOUT MATCHES AND COOKING WITHOUT POTS

IT is often of interest to boys to make a fire in the primitive way: by friction; perhaps to produce the "new fire" for some ceremonial occasion, or it may be to win honors as a scout. If a boy is fond of wilderness camping, it is possible that such knowledge may prove of vital importance to him some day, for even the experienced woodsman may be caught out without matches, or may get his matches wet.

This is the way the Indians made fire before they obtained matches or flint and steel from the white man, and the way I have many times done it myself as a boy. For tools you need a block, a drill, a bow, a socket, and some tinder, dry punk, or cat-tail down, all of which you can make or find in the woods.

For the first, take a smooth piece of pine board, cedar, basswood, cottonwood, or any other wood, but these are soft and

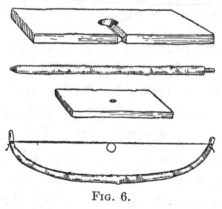

easy to work. It should be a foot long by two inches wide and about half an inch in thickness. Make a round hole or pit in the

FIG. 6.

center half through the board. From this hole cut a notch or groove to the edge of the board.

For the drill, take a hard wood stick about a foot long, whittled down at both ends to fit the hole in block. A piece of wood two by six inches with a hole halfway through its thickness to fit the upper end of the drill forms the socket.

If you have no bow with you, make one of any limber stick two feet long, with a loose buckskin or other thong.

Now put a little tinder — shredded birch-bark or dry pine-needles — along the groove in your block and especially at its upper end. Adjust your fire-maker, wind the bowstring once about the drill, place a foot on each end of the block while your left hand supports and presses down

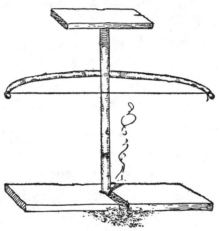

Fig. 7.

on the socket, and your right saws with the bowstring, causing the drill to revolve rapidly in the hole. This friction in time produces smoke and then sparks, which, when you blow upon them, ignite the tinder. It is then only a matter of sufficient dry bark and kindling to make a good fire. You cannot fail after a little practice, if you follow directions carefully. Mr. Seton's record time for making fire in this way is thirty-one seconds, but it will be more likely to take you from one to three minutes, even after you have experimented a little.

The Indian or expert woodsman is never at a loss for dry fire material in the wettest woods. He knows how to look for the *inside* bark of the birch and the *inside* of dead stumps and logs; and a good fire, once kindled, will burn on even under discouraging circumstances.

Indian methods of cookery are of interest in camp, more particularly if the common utensils have been dispensed with as too cumbersome to carry. Neither pots, pans, nor dishes are essential to a good meal in the woods. Berries, some roots, smoked or sun-dried meats may be eaten raw, also eggs, though the latter are preferred cooked by the Indian. He is especially fond of turtle eggs, which are buried in the sand along the lake shores and may be found by searching for them with a pole in the spring.

The simplest method of cooking thin pieces of meat is by broiling over a bed of live coals, upon a long-handled pronged stick or fork of green wood. The meat is turned as often as necessary and is perfectly done in a few minutes.

Roasting is done by spitting your haunch of venison or other large piece of meat upon a stick two to four feet long and sharpened at both ends. This may be thrust into the ground at the right distance from the blaze and turned occasionally, or suspended over the fire from a cross-bar of green wood by a hooked stick, or " planked " against a flat rock inclined toward a hot fire.

The only method of boiling known to the Indian before the white man came with iron and copper kettles was crude but very ingenious, and is known as " stone-boiling." We dug a hole in which we placed a dozen or more round stones of medium size, and over these we built a good fire. About the hole in a square we drove four forked sticks of green wood, and from these suspended a square piece of tripe or rawhide, cutting a small hole in each corner to admit the prong of the support. This bag-kettle was then half filled with water. The heat of the fire soon contracted it, and from time to time a red-hot stone was lifted from the fire and dropped into the water by means of two sticks. When the water boiled, we put in a small piece of meat, and by adding now and then another piece and a hot stone, and taking out the meat as fast as cooked, a savory boil was produced. We liked starchy roots or spicy leaves boiled with our meat, and of these we had a variety to choose from. We had also wild rice and hulled corn, but no bread.

When you wish to hunt or to leave camp for any length of time while your meal is cooking, none of these methods will do and you had better resort to casing the food in wet clay and burying fairly deep in ashes or sand under a good fire. If you have birds it is only necessary to wet the feathers thoroughly before burying them, and they will come out juicy and delicious under a black coat that peels off like the skin of an onion. Fish cooks perfectly in this manner, as do potatoes, green corn, shell fish — in fact, almost anything. It should be done in two or three hours, but you may leave it all day if necessary without harm.

Every camper or Boy Scout should familiarize himself with all the edible roots, herbs, fruits, and fungi in his locality. Lives have been saved by this knowledge, especially in the north woods. Lichens and the inner bark of certain trees are "famine foods," eaten by Indian and white man when hunger presses and no other food is to be found.

The Indian method of preserving fresh

meat in summer by " jerking," or cutting in thin strips and drying on poles in the sun (no salt being needed), is useful only on the high central plains where the air is dry. All kinds of berries and wild fruits are easily sun-dried for future use.

The " cache," an Indian custom estensively copied by white hunters and trappers, is the concealment of reserve stores of food, usually in a hole in the ground, protected by an inner wrapping of bark or rawhide. The mouth of the " cache " is well hidden by building a fire over it, or by covering with rocks, brush, dry leaves, or sand, according to the locality.

XI

HOW TO MAKE AND FOLLOW A BLAZED TRAIL

THE blazed trail is especially designed for those who travel in the deep woods, where these simple guide-posts are necessary at times, if only for temporary use. The Indian hunter sometimes finds himself with a limited time in which to provide his winter's supply of meat, before the opening of the trapping season. In such an event, he would not take time to carry all his game home, but would blaze connecting trails to where he had killed and hung up the different animals, and a direct road home. There is also the trapper's trail, the regular path between established camps, and the concealed or secret blazed trail. We

shall consider each of these varieties in
order.

The blazed trail meant for general use
— the public highway, as it were — may
not always be the shortest road, but it
will be the easiest and most convenient.
You may blaze such a trail to the moun-
tain-top for the finest view, or to your
cabin in the woods. The blazes on the
trees will be obvious and near together,
about three inches long and three feet
from the ground. At every turn a sapling
is felled, at the same height as the blaze,
the felled top hanging on its stump and
pointing in the desired direction.

The game trail differs from the above
in several respects. The blazes are smaller
and are about five feet high; they are also
further apart — about twenty to twenty-
five paces. At each turn the hack is deeper,
and if to the left, it is made on the left
side of the tree, if to the right, on the right
side. The blazes are more open to view
when coming from the camp, as when the

scout has gone over it once, he can always follow it back home. An Indian game trail is very indistinct to one who is not looking for it, and even then it requires training to follow it readily. To one who is a thoroughly competent woodsman, each mark is a real blaze of light, quite unmistakable.

If you wish to blaze a trail correctly, you must place your mark accurately on the right tree and on the right side of the tree. You should not disfigure the trees, and you will not, if you do your work as well as the Indian. If you go about gashing them indiscriminately, your work will be an eyesore, and besides, everybody will know your trail. It should be just enough guide for your friends, neatly done, and courting no unnecessary publicity.

The trapper's trail is one more degree nearer a concealed blaze. It is blazed on each noteworthy tree, twenty to thirty paces apart, and even higher than the game trail. At a point opposite the first trap, there is a peculiar hack, a double hack, or a twig clipped, varying with the code of the individual. In any case, you are directed toward the lake shore or river bank, where you find an upright stick broken off two feet from the ground and bent over until it touches the water. This means the trap is in the water. If the broken part does not reach the water, it means look for it on shore, and if a birch-bark ring is added, it means the trap is in a hole. At each point a certain sign leads you approximately near the trap, where you get a hint as to its closer whereabouts.

This kind of trail does not begin at the camp, but at a point which may be orally described, in case the trapper is unable to visit his traps and must send his wife or some member of his family. He then entrusts the messenger with his personal code, which sometimes includes the sign for the animal he is trapping.

The concealed blaze is used by a party

on the war-path, so that another war-party of the same tribe may overtake them or discover their camp. It was not usual to blaze a war-path unless another party was likely to follow. In such a contingency, the first party leaves an occasional blaze high up on the tree and pointing in the direction in which they are traveling. Such blazes are only made at well-known points and are looked for by those who come after. When the high blaze is found, other information is sought for, which may be given by means of signs or hicroglyphics in a concealed place.

If a party of boys are out for a hike over roads which are not well known, and there are stragglers, the leader may indicate the trail by Indian signs. At the cross-roads he may tie a bunch of grass to a low branch on the right side of the road he takes. If he leaves the path entirely, he must stick up a rod with a knot of grass tied to the top, bending it in the right direction. If at any point he desires to return and meet the others, he breaks two opposite twigs toward one another, as a sign in case he misses them. If he wishes his party to camp there, he draws a circle on the ground. This system is used a great deal by the Indians when two or three families are roving together in the deep woods, hunting or trapping game. When there is only one family, and they are within the danger-line from tribal enemies, the hunter uses a concealed blaze for his wife to follow, and he may adopt a special code whose meaning is known to no one but the two. When he wishes to be particularly obscure, he makes his blaze inside a group of trees. It is a right-angled gash pointing straight to the next blaze.

I remember that I was once instructed to follow a hunter's trail, together with several other boys. We were in the country of the Crees, who were at war with us; but game was abundant, and there was no better location, therefore our hunters took extra chances of danger. However, every precaution was observed.

One of our men had killed a moose late in the afternoon, and on the next morning we boys were instructed to find it and bring home the meat. The first blaze was perhaps half a mile from our camp, on the inside of one of four large birch trees. Above the blaze were two hacks, and above this the mark of an arrow-head. This meant to follow the blaze two hundred paces in the direction of the arrow, and then search for another mark. The next arrow pointed diagonally toward the lake, and two hundred paces further we came out upon the lake shore. We followed the shore to a conspicuous tree, upon the bark of which we discovered a small blaze and the figure of an animal. About fifty paces from this last blaze, we found the moose.

In a prairie country, where there are no trees, stones are piled upon the hills or buttes in a manner to give information to those who come after. Many of these large boulders or cone-shaped heaps of stones were discovered in the prairie states when settlement was made, and some well-known ones have been preserved for many years as historic landmarks.

We Indians never stand boldly out upon a hilltop without having first lain flat and surveyed the country from a concealed position to see that no danger is in sight. We then place the stones so as to convey intelligence to our friends. One is placed with the apex pointing in the direction in which the traveler is going, and several more behind the main pile show from whence he came. If he has seen signs of the enemy, he places two small stones on either side of the central stone. If he cannot go further, he puts these in front of the central one, meaning an obstacle in the path, or reverses the three on the opposite side, meaning that he will return. An old stone pile may be used again and again by slightly displacing the stones. This is the prairie " blazed trail."

XII

INDIAN SIGNALS IN CAMP AND FIELD

IN the early and free life of the North American Indian, he was constantly in motion, the various bands of each tribe covering a large area during the year. The hunters, travelers, and war-parties of these widely scattered bands had their well-known codes of signals in the field and on the trail, by means of which it was possible to communicate from a distance. The methods in common use were the smoke, mirror, and blanket signals, all of which could be more readily practiced by the Plains Indians than by those of the woods, for obvious reasons.

There are three distinct kinds of intelligence given in this manner, which may be thus described: First, warning of danger;

second, sighting of game; third, general news of importance from another tribe or village. Any person who happens to be in the field and discovers the approach of danger must instantly signal a warning by any means in his power. If he is in full view of the camp or of the individual whom he desires to reach, the blanket method is used.

A blanket or other article of clothing tightly rolled and held with outstretched arms so as to form, with the body, a cross or a capital T, is the primary danger-signal. If the person signaling runs to and fro, it means that the danger is approaching, and if, in addition to these, the blanket is thrown horizontally, it is a call for rescue or signal of immediate distress.

When game is sighted, the game scout runs to and fro; that means a small herd of game, especially buffalo. If he runs in a circle, tossing up his blanket, it denotes a large herd. If he runs back and forth with blanket trailing behind, it indicates

bad news. The blanket held straight
above the head signifies important tidings
from a distance.

Since the mirror came into use among
us, each warrior carries with him a small
round reflector. With this it is easy to
flash a signal into the camp or toward the
surrounding hills, upon which it is customary to keep a continual lookout. One
long flash is the signal for attention, and
as soon as it is answered, you may give
the message to be transmitted. One short
flash means that game is in sight. Two
short flashes means the enemy is in sight.
Two short flashes followed by one long
one is a call for rescue. Two short flashes
and one long followed by two more short
flashes means the danger is over. Four
short flashes signifies a meeting with a
stranger or news from a distance.

The smoke signal is resorted to when
no other could be employed, on account
of distance or obstacles in the way, such
as hills or forest. As this is a long-distance

signal, the codes vary among different
tribes, so that the intelligence conveyed
may not be of equal advantage to the foe.
Among the Sioux, it was often used by
war-parties, announcing their return and
giving news of success or failure; the number of scalps or horses taken might also
be indicated.

To make this signal, you must build a
brisk fire upon some convenient knoll,
and as soon as it is burning freely, smother
it with coarse green grass, also heap earth
around it so that the smoke may be dense
and closely confined. When it has burned
long enough to gain attention, check
the smoke for an instant by holding a
blanket over the fire and then withdrawing
it, causing a succession of short puffs,
with intervals between. To avoid confusion; it will be well to adopt the code
given above for mirror flashes. At night,
a signal fire is sometimes kindled. Since
fire is not always easy to control single-
handed, the Indian is careful to turn up

the earth before he builds his fire, and to
have an abundance of green grass at hand,
not only to produce a sufficient volume
of smoke, but to put the fire out if necessary.

The drum is used for home communications. When four measured blows are
struck, followed by many short ones, it
is a call to the council. If every warrior
is not present at the second signal, given
a few minutes after the first, the Indian
" soldiers " or police will come after the
absentees. At all dances, the drum is
used to call the dancers together, the third
call being accompanied by yelps and the
fourth by a real burst of war-whoops.
There is a curious variation in the call
to the scalp dance, which is something
like skipping a stone on new ice. It begins
in slow time, with each successive beat
shorter, and ending in a mere roll.

There are also many signal calls exe-
cuted by the voice alone, such as the call
to war, the journey and hunting halloos,

the good deed calls, and other yodels or musical shouts which are very effective and may be heard at a considerable distance.

XIII

G AMES with arrows are the most popular Indian sports. If you are camping in the woods, you may like to play the " Tree Game."

About a dozen blunt or knob-headed arrows are shot up into the branches of a large, wide-spreading tree, in such a manner that they are all caught and hang there in many different positions. Then, at a given signal, the boys begin to shoot them down. Every arrow that a boy brings down is his; each one of his own that gets lodged becomes a " prize arrow " for the others to shoot at. Now and then an arrow hugs the limb so closely that it can hardly be seen; eventually all the boys aim at this one, and if they are so unlucky

as to lose their own arrows without bringing it down, the " tree wins."

Wand games are very simple and are
played by the younger boys. The wands
are from four to six feet long and as big
round as a man's little finger. They are
merely peeled switches of any kind of
shrub, usually the common red willow.
To decorate in Indian fashion, you must
take off with a sharp knife a long strip
of bark; then, having scraped off all the
rest, wind your ribbon of bark spirally
round the peeled wand. After fastening
each end securely, hold it over a smudge
fire until it is well smoked. Then remove
the strip and you will find a spiral of white
against the deep yellow of the uncovered
wood. Sometimes two strips are wound
in opposite directions, leaving yellow diamonds bordered with white.

The wand is pitched and made to strike
at the start upon an inclined mound or a
low horizontal bar, from which it should
bound with much force and sail through

the air like an arrow, sometimes as far as fifty yards. A simple way to give it momentum is to raise the left foot as high as the right knee, rest the side of the wand against the left instep and propel it vigorously.

From two to a dozen boys choose sides. The side winning the toss sends the first wand, and the other side follows, each boy playing in turn for as long as they fail to pass the first. When they succeed in passing it, the first party tries again, and the game continues until one side has spent all its wands, which are gathered up by the winners. Enthusiastic partisans indulge in cheering, dancing and singing to encourage their friends and confuse and dishearten the opposite party, but are not allowed to interfere in any way with the players.

Wand games are played properly in the summer-time; their winter substitutes are the "snow-snake" and "ground arrow." The former is used only on fresh snow.

It is a flat stick five feet long and about
an inch and a half wide at the widest point,
gradually tapering to half that width at
the " tail " end. The head and neck curve
slightly upward and are painted to look
as much like those of a snake as possible;
the body of the wand is polished and hard-
ened by fire. The Indian boy hurls this
mimic serpent into the loose, light snow,

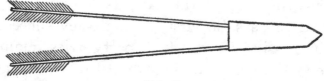

FIG. 8.

where it disappears, to appear again some
distance off; again it dives beneath the
surface only to come up again, somewhat
like skipping a stone on water. The winner
is he who can make it travel farthest.

Ground arrows are of two kinds. One
kind, called " mechá," is made of the
short ribs of buffalo or beef cattle. The
rib is cut off four inches from the free end,
and two small holes bored, into which

sticks, the size of a lead-pencil and about
a foot in length, are tightly inserted. The
end·of each is feathered like an arrow, and
they spread out so that the feathered
shafts are perhaps nine inches apart. The
whole looks much like the white boy's
shuttlecock.

This "mechá" is grasped firmly between the projecting shafts, and thrown
against a little mound the size of a pillow,
made of snow dampened and packed solidly.
From this it rebounds, sails off like a bird,
strikes the hard crust to bound up again
and again, and finally crawls along like a
wounded animal. The goal, which is called
the "blanket goal," is an oblong about
six by ten paces in size, drawn on the snow
at some fifty yards' distance. Lengthwise
of this oblong are drawn six lines, with
seven spaces between. The outer spaces
count two, the next four, the next eight,
and the center space counts sixteen, if
your "mechá" hits it in one throw. Any
number may play the game.

The other kind of ground arrow, called " matká," is shaped like an arrow. It is made of hard wood in one piece, and is about two feet long with a cone-shaped

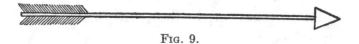

Fig. 9.

head, burnt and polished to look like horn. The shaft must be limber, and carries a small tuft of feathers to guide it in its flight. Another arrow shows an attached

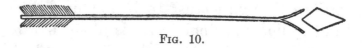

Fig. 10.

head of elk or buffalo horn, which is better than wood.

The boys throw this in the same manner as the " mechá," but the course is laid out more elaborately, with obstacles, such as ravines and small hillocks, and a series of five rings each ten feet in diameter, composed of five concentric circles with a " bull's-eye " in the center. Beside each ring there is a snow mound from which to propel the arrow.

The game is in some ways like golf, and may be played individually or by sides, each player having two strokes in which to reach the next ring, the first a distance throw and the second a push or shove in the direction of the ring. The outer circle counts one, and each inner circle doubles the count, the bull's-eye counting thirty-two. All the players play in turn, starting from the snow mound nearest the ring where their arrows lie at the beginning of each round. The score is added at the close of the game, the boy or team with the highest number of points being the winner.

This is perhaps the most popular and exciting winter sport for Indian boys ten years of age and upward. Sometimes they send the arrow flying a hundred yards before touching the ground, and half as far again at the first rebound, after which it continues for several shorter flights.

The rings are two hundred to three hundred yards apart for young men, or half that distance for small boys; the game may be played on snow-covered lakes or rivers as well as in the open country.

XIV

A MONG the really absorbing amuse-
ments of Indian boys, none sur-
pass the games played with tops,
which with us are in season in the winter
only. The mere spinning of a top would
soon become tiresome; it is the various and
ingenious stunts that keep the interest
alive.

Then, too, each boy makes his own top
of every available kind of wood, as well
as of horn and bone, and studies its peculiar defects or advantages for the work in
hand, so thoroughly that it comes to have
for him a kind of personality. He whittles
it to a nicety in the regular top shape or
any variation of it that he chooses, so
long as he can coax and whip it into spin-

ning and humming and singing. He has
a stick about a foot long and as big as
your thumb; sometimes one end is grooved
so that he can pick up the top while spinning. To this stick he ties two or three
deer-skin thongs of equal length, making
a top whip with which he performs some
interesting stunts and plays many amu-
sing games.

There is much artistic taste among our
people. Some decorate their tops in stripes,
much like a barber's pole; others with
totem paintings; but perhaps the cleverest
boy is he who can carve as well as paint.
One will carve a tiny toad sitting atop
his spinner; another a turtle; but the boy
who is quick enough to copy the bumble-
bee — hum and all — he is a hero! When
he proudly whips his black buffalo-horn
spinner, he holds the center of the stage,
while every other boy must pause for a
minute to regard him with envy.

Sometimes a boy will playfully address
his top, telling it to sing the bear song, or

imitate the lowing of the buffalo bull, at
the same time whipping it so vigorously
and in such fashion that it seems really
to give a semblance of the required imitation! But it is no ordinary bashful boy
who does these things; it is the roguish
young humorist and actor of the tribe.

When the chiefs selected for our field-
day on the ice announce the date, every
boy is ready. The chief of each side brings
his forces together for a final test of skill,
and there is no lack of spectators. In the
first place, each displays his peculiar man-
ufactures, priding himself much upon orig-
inality of design and careful workmanship.
Then there are trials of speed, and trials
of duration, and finally the more difficult
stunts, such as transferring the top in the
spoon end of the whip without interrupt-
ing its dance, or whipping it under a light
covering of snow, or along an obstacle
course. Perhaps no one save an Indian
could make a bear cub whip a spinning-
top, holding the whip handle in his mouth,

as I have seen it done on these field-days. Some of the boys impersonate old men, and some genuine grandfathers are admitted to add to the fun. There is a particular song of the top, and its spinning is said by us to be symbolic of the dance of life.

A white boy feels himself unfortunate when Santa Claus fails to leave at his home a pair of club skates or a swift " flexible flyer." Still more unfortunate is he who has no hill or pond or river near for coasting and skating. In my day we were independent of all save natural features; no policeman to interfere with our fun, no fences or trespass signs — and no shops or indulgent fathers to purchase our equipment! The trees might be snapping, even bursting open with the severe cold, the ice on the lakes thundering like the cannonade of a distant battle, but, nothing daunted, we boys would sally forth in our warm buffalo calf-skin robes, well belted around the middle, and moccasins stuffed

with hair, defying the weather. Our coast-
ers were made of the longest and largest
ribs of the buffalo bull, tightly bound together with strong rawhide thongs, and
held in position with three flat sticks an
inch or two wide and a little longer than
the width of the sled. The shape was something like the body of a cutter; it was lined
neatly with buffalo hide, and lariats were
tied to the curved end as you tie your
ropes. We generally coasted standing
erect, and the narrower ones were used
as skees, with a pole to balance, upon
which we sped like lightning down the
steep hills amid a din of yells, whoops,
and laughter. Other skees were made of
basswood or elm bark, stiffened with rawhide or doubled, always with the slippery
inner side against the snow. In the very
old days there were a kind of skates of
peculiar workmanship, made of bones and
tusks of animals.

The winter pageant or winter masque
on the ice was the crowning event, and

here the older people came to realize how
closely they had been watched and studied
by their children. Your Indian boy is a
born mimic and impersonator, and this
was his day. The first intimation of the
festivity was given by their crier or herald,
who entered the camp picturesquely attired, riding on a tame buffalo calf or a
big Esquimo dog, announcing the coming
of the " old folks " or the " first people."

When the whole village had poured
forth from their wigwams in eager expecta-
tion, the head of the procession emerged
from the forest upon the field of ice. It
was an imposing sight. The first clan,
perhaps, would be led by a buffalo bull
walking upright and holding his pipe in
his hands like a man. Immediately behind him were twelve wise men walking
abreast, each wearing a buffalo headdress
and carrying a long staff with a buffalo-
tail tassel. They were followed by the
people of the clan, all clad in hairy skins,
some accompanied by tame coyotes, or

dragging old-time travois. Here and there, boys in groups were playing their favorite games or fluting and yodeling, while the groups of pretty girls walked more demurely.

The wolf, elk, and bear clans were similarly represented, and the odd characters of ancient legend were all present: Unktómee the tricky one with his many aliases; Heyóka the contrary one, who always says the reverse of what he means, and paints a face or mask on the back of his head so that he seems to be walking backward. Even his dog wears the head of a calf at his rear end, and a tail fixed on the end of his nose. One figure is dressed all in white and moves with a whirling motion, all the time imitating the humming of a top. Even the wild pets join in the fun, and I have heard a tame crow, which had been taught a few simple words, crying out quite naturally as he hopped along: "Wachée po! wachée po!" (Dance, friends, dance!)

XV

AN INDIAN GIRL'S SPORTS

CONTRARY to the popular opinion,
our Indian girls and women are
not mere drudges, but true feminine athletes, almost as alert as the men,
and frequently even more muscular.

The favorite outdoor sport of the plains-
women from remote times is called by
them "tap-káp-see-cha," the original form
of "field hockey." Any level prairie ground
is suited to the game, which is especially
exciting when it is engaged in by two neighboring camps. The goals are usually two
hundred yards apart, and the width of the
ground about twenty feet. Twenty-five
to fifty or more contestants may play on
each side, but not all at once. They are
placed in groups or relays, each group not

to go beyond its allotted field. When a ball crosses the line, it belongs to the next group. Thus, if there are fifty players on a side, each group of ten runs only forty yards.

The ball, which is of buckskin, about as large as a baseball, but softer, is tossed up with a war-whoop, midway between the goals. Each side then strives to send it on with their hooked sticks toward the opposing goal. It may either be kept rolling along the ground, or driven through the air; and the battle continues until one side or the other succeeds in sending it over the enemy's goal. The distinctive features of the Indian game are the apportionment of the field to designated groups of players, and the large number taking part, thus reducing the confusion and chances of accident while ensuring an exceedingly picturesque and lively spectacle.

" Pas-ló-han " is played in smaller groups with a wand about eight feet long, heavy

at the forward end, which is shaped somewhat like the head of a snake, and tapering gently to about the size of a man's
finger. Sometimes the head is made of
buffalo, elk, or deer's horn. The girls
hold it between the thumb, middle, and
ring fingers, while the index finger presses
against the end. The arm is closely bent
at the elbow and held at right angles to
the body, bringing the half-opened hand
directly over the shoulder, and the wand
is then hurled with all the strength of the
player's arm, two or three forward steps
being taken at the same time. The head
hits the ground slantwise, and the body
slides and wriggles after it much like a
fleeing snake. The immediate object of
the girls, who throw in turn, is to see who
can make it go furthest, but grace and
swiftness of flight are also points to be
considered.

This simple sport brings into use prac-
tically all the muscles that are required to
throw a baseball, and helps much to make

the girls supple and agile. It is easier to play in winter and late fall, as the wands travel much faster over crusty snow or hard-trampled ground.

The Minnesota Sioux used to play a very pretty aquatic game when their homes were in that beautiful lake country. It was really the original Indian game of lacrosse played in birch-bark canoes, and might be christened " water lacrosse " or " canoe ball."

The ball was twice as large as the one the men used on land; I should say a little larger than a baseball, but much lighter in weight. The sticks used by the Sioux women were about like the ordinary lacrosse stick, only a foot longer and with twice as large a pocket. This pocket is made of vegetable fiber so that the wet does not stretch it, and when the ball is in it, barely one-third shows above the rim.

Ten to twenty girls may play on a side, two to each canoe. We will designate them "ball-player" and "canoeist." The latter must devote herself entirely to her canoe and that of her opponent. She may not touch the ball nor interfere with the opposing ball-player, but she may use all her skill to obstruct the opposing canoe, and if her partner secures the ball, it is her duty to guard against being thus obstructed. In a skirmish she must be skilful and alert to balance her craft. No canoeist may ram her opponent head on, and if she does so, the game is given to the other side.

The ball-player must throw the ball to one of her own side if possible. Here again special skill is required, for it is nearly as difficult as making a successful "forward pass." However, she has the privilege of passing it in any direction to one of her own players. It is not allowable to hit the ball while in the water. Each player may carry it on toward her opponent's goal so long as her canoe is not obstructed, but as soon as her bows are crossed, she must pass it on. Thus the

struggle continues until the ball either
goes out of bounds, or passes over one of
the goals. The field is about a hundred
yards long by fifty wide. If the ball goes
out of bounds, the referee must toss it up
as at the beginning, in the middle of the
field between two opposing canoes, the
canoeists placing the canoes parallel to
each other, while the players struggle for
the possession of the ball. Meanwhile,
the other players occupy strategic points
and hold themselves ready to receive it.

In this feminine game, it is forbidden
to throw the ball with a full arm swing;
it must be lobbed or tossed with the forearm only, to avoid risk of injury to the
players. It develops much nicety of physical equilibrium, and might be successfully
revived in a summer camp by girls who
are good swimmers. They would do well
to wear bathing-suits and be fully prepared for the chances of an upset. In our
day, the winners were entertained by the
conquered side at a simple feast.

XVI

INDIAN NAMES AND THEIR SIGNIFICANCE

A S you all know, we Indians had no books; our history and traditions were orally preserved. The pictograph cut into a rock or tree, or painted upon a buffalo-skin tent, was our only record of current or past events. Moreover, we had no family names, so that a boy's name did not indicate his parentage. Under such circumstances, one should have a striking cognomen in order to be readily identified.

The Sioux had three classes of names; first, birth names; second, honor or public names; third, nicknames. The first indicated the order 'in which children were born into the family; as " Chaskáy," first-born son, " Wenónah," first-born daughter, and so on to the fifth child, who was presumed to be the last. There were a few who carried this childhood name through life.

The nickname usually records some humorous act or odd characteristic of the boy or man. It is seldom a flattering one. There is an imaginary Indian personage called "Wink'tah," who is supposed to be ever on the watch for an excuse to coin a ridiculous or insinuating name, and such a one will travel like a prairie fire before its owner is aware of it.

It has been written by white men that an Indian child is called after the first noticeable thing its mother sees after its birth. This is not so as a rule, though it is possible such cases may have occurred. Again, it has been declared that some event occurring near the child's birth establishes its name. This occasionally happens, but only when the event is of unusual importance.

The child's " honor name " is properly

conferred by the clan medicine-man at a
public ceremony, some time after the
child is able to walk. Such an Indian
christening is announced by the herald,
a feast made, and gifts presented to the
poor of the tribe, in honor of the occasion.
These needy old people in their turn go
away singing the praises of the child by
his new name.

Such a name usually indicates the distinguishing character or famous deeds of
the boy's ancestors, and its bearer is ex-
pected to live up to, defend, and pass it
on, unstained. Through this ancient custom, he is early recognized by his tribe,
impressed with a sense of his personal
responsibility, and inspired with the ambition to be worthy of his ancestry. By
giving away their property to those in
want, his parents intend to teach him
love and good-will toward his fellow-men.
But if, when he grows up, the boy fails
to sustain his honor name, he is no longer
called by it.

If he does not fail, but on the other hand performs some special deed of valor, or wins some distinguished honor on his own account, he may later be given a special " deed name," and the conferring of such was at one time strictly guarded among the Sioux. Our unwritten book of " Who's Who " is composed of just such heroes.

The deed name is generally given by the war chief, and such naming is not accompanied by gifts. A deed requiring great physical courage is often celebrated by giving the name of some fear-inspiring animal, such as Bear or Buffalo, or one of the nobler bird names — those of Eagle, Hawk, and Owl. The character of the exploit, calling for special strength, swiftness, agility, or endurance, helps to determine the name chosen, or adds a qualifying word descriptive of some poetic or picturesque quality in the action. Examples are " Charging Eagle " and " Conquering Bear."

Not only bird and animal names, but those of the elements, are commonly used to express temperament. The rash, impetuous man may be called "Storm," or "Whirlwind." Loftiness and beauty of character is indicated by a name including the word "sky," or "cloud," such as "Red Cloud," "Touch-the-Cloud," "Blue Sky," or "Hole-in-the-Day," all names of well-known chiefs. Sometimes the idea of bravery or swiftness conveyed by the name of animal or bird is combined with another suggestive of dignity, sacredness, mystery, or magic; as, for example, "Thunder Bear," or "Spirit Buffalo."

The highest type of brave deed name is represented by "Thunder," or "Lightning," in one of its many variations. "Crazy Bull" and "Crazy Horse" stand for utter fearlessness and unconsciousness of danger, rather than madness. Resourcefulness, generosity, and productiveness are expressed in the name of "Earth" with some of its poetic attributes. "Fire" represents daring and war-like qualities. Colors are used in a purely symbolic sense, thus redeeming from any touch of absurdity such names as " Red Wolf " and " Black Eagle."

Many Indian names have been roughly handled in translation by illiterate persons, such as were most of the early interpreters. The raven was a dignified bird which disappeared with the buffalo, but its name is generally mistranslated as crow. The Sioux call the crow the " scolding grandmother," and use its name only as a satirical jest. The famous chief known as " Young-man-afraid-of-his-Horses," was really called " Man-whose-Horse-is-feared " (by the enemy).

An instance of the highly poetic and figurative name is that of " Wee-yó-tank-ah-loó-tah." Literally translated, it means " He who in his usual home-going pauses upon an eminence glowing with scarlet light." The reference is to the Sun, who, at the close of his day's journey across the prairies of the sky, apparently rests for a moment upon his gorgeous seat at the verge of the horizon. He who bears that name needs no introduction; its beauty is eloquence enough.

Here are some honor names for Boy Scouts.

Wam-blee'-skah.	White Eagle.
Ta-tonk'-ah-sap'-ah.	Black Buffalo.
Mah-to'-skah.	White Bear.
Chay-ton'-ho-tah.	Gray Falcon.
Chay-ton'-wah-koo'-wah.	Charging Falcon.
Kan-gee'-loo-tah.	Red Raven.
Kan-gee-'wah-kan.	Sacred Raven.
Mah-kah'-skah.	White Earth.
Mah-pee'-yah-to.	Blue Sky.
Mah-pee'-yah-loo'-tah.	Red Sky (or Cloud).
Wah-kan'-glee-o'-ta.	Many Lightnings.
Tah-tay'-an-pah.	Wind, or Storm.
O-han'-zee.	Shadow (Comforting).
Pay'-tah.	Fire.
Tah-wah'-soo-o'-ta.	His Hailstorm (Forcible, or Impetuous).
We-hin'-ah-pay.	Rising Sun.
We'-e-yah-yah.	Setting Sun.
Ah-kee'-chee-tah.	Soldier.
O-hit'-e-kah.	Brave.
Wan'-ah-ton.	Charger.
O'-tak-tay.	Kills or Strikes Many.
Tee-tonk'-ah.	Big Lodge.
Chank-oo'-wash-tay.	Good Road.

Nah-pay'-shnee.	He does not flee (Courageous).
E'-nap-ay.	Comes Out (Appears Bravely).
Wah-chin'-tonk-ah.	Patient.
Wah-chink'-sap-ah.	Wise, Clear-headed.
Tah-ko'-dah.	Friend to them all.
O-dah'-ko-tah.	Friendly.
Tah-o'-han-o'-tah.	His Many Good Deeds.
Tah-wah'-hink-pay-o'-tah.	His Many Arrows (Resourceful).
Ko-han'-nah.	Swift.
O'-gal-lee-shah.	Red Shirt.
Ho'-wah-kan.	Mysterious Voice.
Wah-nah'-gee-skah.	White Spirit.
Wah-nee'-kee-yah.	Savior.
Wah-hah'-chank-ah.	Shield.

XVII

INDIAN GIRLS' NAMES AND SYMBOLIC
DECORATIONS

ALL Indian art is symbolic, and the
decorative native designs may be
so applied in bead-work, basketry,
weaving, embroidery, or jewelry as to express the ideals and personality of the
maker. This is true of all the tribes, but
the individual symbols vary
with their customs and habitat.

In all genuine Sioux handiwork, the central design is the
isosceles triangle (Fig. 11),

FIG. 11.   representing the conical teepee
or tent — the home. This is used in many
different ways. Two tents with the bases
united, forming a diamond (Fig. 12), indicate the four points of the compass, or the

whole world. Two tents with the peaks
together (Fig. 13) are symbolic of life here

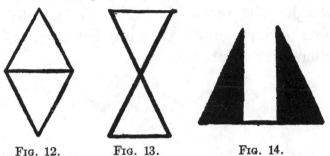

FIG. 12.   FIG. 13.   FIG. 14.

and hereafter. The dark tent cut in half
with a band of white, yellow, or light blue
in the center (Fig. 14) signifies happiness

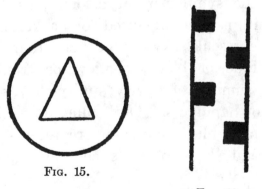

FIG. 15.

FIG. 16

in the home. The tent enclosed in a circle
(Fig. 15) means eternal union.

Figure 16 is commonly used to represent footprints or man's trail through the
world. The zig-zag line (Fig. 17) is lightning or destruction; the wavy line (Fig. 18)
mountains or prayer.

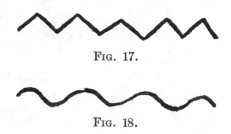

FIG. 17.

FIG. 18.

In the symbolism of colors, pale blue
or white is generally used for background,
and represents sky or heaven; red, life;
dark blue or black, shadow or trouble;
green, summer or plenty; and yellow, sun-
light or happiness. Dark blue, dovetailed
with pale blue or yellow, represents the
light and shade of life's common experience.

Animal figures are much used in conventionalized designs. The figure of the
bear means courage; the buffalo, plenty;

the eagle (wings spread), honor; the owl,
observation; the wolf, skill; the turtle,
wisdom and longevity; the serpent, healing; the hawk, swiftness; the beaver, industry; the deer, love. The figure of a
man on horseback represents a warrior.

No Indian girl may wear the skin or
any representation of the bear, wolf, or
cat, nor wear the feathers of the eagle,
since these are masculine emblems. The
doe, ermine, otter, and mink are feminine
emblems.

It is usually possible to distinguish feminine from masculine personal names by
the meaning. The names of the fiercer
wild animals, such as bear, wolf, and eagle,
are given to boys; girls are called after
the fawn, mink, beaver, etc. Either may
be called after sky, wind, or water, but
the name of Fire is masculine. The sylla-
ble "wee" is a feminine termination.
"Na" is a diminutive, used much like
"ie" in English.

The following are Sioux feminine names

appropriate to " Camp Fire girls," with their literal and symbolic meanings.

Wee-no'-nah.	Eldest Daughter. Loaf-giver, charitable.
Wee-hah'-kay-dah.	Youngest Daughter. Little One.
War-chah'-wash-tay.	Pretty Flower. Beautiful.
O-jin'-jint-kah.	Rose. Queen of Flowers.
Zit-kah'-lah-skah.	White Bird. Pure.
Do'-wan-ho'-wee.	Singing Voice.
Wa-chee'-wee.	Dancing Girl.
Han-tay'-wee.	Cedar Maid. Faithful.
Wa-zee'-me-nah-wee.	Odors of the Pine. Wholesome, refreshing.
Mah-kah'-wee.	Earth Maiden. Generous, motherly.
Mah-pee'-yah.	Sky. Heavenly.
E-ha'-wee.	Laughing Maid.
Wee-ko'.	Pretty Girl.
Ptay-san'-wee.	White Buffalo. Queen of the Herd.
Mah-gah'-skah-wee.	Swan Maiden. Graceful.
Wah-su'-lah.	Little Hail-storm. Stormy, impulsive.
Snah'-nah.	Jingles (like little bells). Musical.
Ta-lu'-tah.	Scarlet. Brilliant.
Ta-tee'-yo-pah.	Her Door. Happy Hostess.
Wee-tash'-nah.	Virgin. Untouched.
Tak-cha'-wee.	Doe. Loving.
Chah'-pah-wee.	Beaver. Industrious.
An-pay'-too.	Day. Radiant.
Wik-mun'-kee-wee.	Rainbow. Return of Blessing.

And some Ojibway girls' names.

Man-e-do-bin'-es.	Spirit Bird, or Bird Spirit.
O-min-o-tah'-go.	Pleasant Voice.
Ke-we-din'-ok.	Woman of the Wind.
A-ya'-she.	Little One.
A-be'-da-bun.	Peep of Day.
Ke-zhe-ko'-ne.	Fire Briskly Burning.
O-dah-ing'-um.	Ripple on the Water.
Me-o-quan'-ee.	Clothed in Red.
Nah-tah'-ak-on.	Expert Canoeist.
She-she'-bens.	Little Duck.
A-be'-qua.	She Stays at Home.

XVIII

IN the first place, the wearing of feathers is not peculiar to the Indians, except in the value attached to them as symbols of character and true worth. Any one may wear any sort of feather as ornament merely, or in imitation of the old-time warrior, but with him it was a serious affair. He adopted only the feathers of certain birds, and these must be worn in accordance with well-understood law and custom.

The following birds are held in especially high honor: namely, the eagle, raven, and falcon, commonly called hawk. But it must be borne in mind that as far as the Indian is concerned, there is only one hawk that holds an honorable position:

that is the American falcon. He is daring
to recklessness in his methods of warfare
and hunting, and though not large, is
swift and graceful. The raven is held
next to the eagle in dignity and wisdom;
and the owl comes next on the roll of
honored birds. Some of the water-fowl,
such as the loon, cormorant, and pelican,
play a minor part in our myths and folk-
lore, but in the warriors' codes and emblems only the dashing and courageous
birds of prey are permitted to appear —
the American eagle standing first.

The feathers of this bird are highly
prized, since they stand for brave deeds
and form a warrior's record. They are
variously worn among different tribes.
Perhaps the best and completest system
was developed by the Sioux nation; a system which was gradually adopted by their
neighbors on the plains, and which I shall
follow closely.

No Sioux may wear an eagle's tail-
feather unless he has counted a *coup*, or

stroke, upon an enemy, dead or alive. If
in a battle, the deed is witnessed by his
fellow-warriors; but if he was alone when
he made the count, he must have unmistakable proof, or the feather is not awarded.
There are four *coup* counts on each enemy,
and these are secured in succession. Even
upon a living enemy, if he is overpowered
and held captive, these four counts could
properly be shared by the warriors. But
it is obvious that in most cases they are
very difficult to secure. A man may strike
an enemy in a hand-to-hand battle, or,
as you would say, in a " mix-up," and he
gets away without being killed or even
seriously hurt. In this case, only one
coup is counted. Again, many foes are
killed upon whose bodies no *coup* at all
is counted, because it is impossible to
obtain, and upon others, one or two may
be taken with much difficulty and superb
daring in the face of the enemy's fire.
Herein lies the relative value of individual
feathers, and the degree of valor shown or

difficulty encountered determines the sub-
sidiary trimmings, tassels, and ornaments.

Primarily, every eagle feather worn by
a warrior represents a *coup* given in battle.
This is important to remember. No other
feather stands for the same thing, though
different degrees of courage and endurance
may be expressed by other feathers.

For instance, a group of raven or of
Canadian goose feathers trimmed on the
sides, indicates that the wearer has been
wounded in battle more than once. A
single goose feather dyed red and trimmed,
means that the wearer was severely
wounded in battle. Sometimes a man
wears an eagle feather dyed or trimmed,
meaning that he was wounded at the time
he counted the *coup*. An eagle feather
notched and the cut dyed red, means that
the wearer counted the *coup* and took the
scalp also, but was wounded while so doing.

He may have the feather cut off at the
tip, showing that he killed his foe and

counted the *coup* on that same enemy. If he fought a desperate battle, with the odds against him, in which he came off victor, he may tip his eagle's feather with buffalo hair; and if he counted *coup* in a charge on horseback in the face of imminent danger, he may tip it with hair from a horse's tail.

Among some tribes, the wearing of a split feather denotes that the wearer has been wounded, and when the feather is clipped off at the tip, that he has taken a scalp. When a warrior wears one eagle feather upright and the rest drooping, it indicates that he was surrounded in company with a party of warriors of whom he was the sole survivor.

As I have said, the Indian might wear as many eagle feathers as he had counted *coups*. When he had won a number of these in difficult circumstances, and had been held at bay and surrounded by the enemy, but succeeded in getting away, he was entitled to a regular war-bonnet. Only an exceptional record of many battles in which he had shown great coolness, skill, and daring, entitled him to the long, trailing war-bonnet of many plumes.

There are other ornaments and portions of a warrior's dress that bear a special significance. If he has been in the vanguard of battle more than once and led counter-charges, he may wear the whole skin of a raven on his back in the dances. If he has pursued his enemy into the hostile camp and killed him there, he may wear an otter skin slit up the middle so that his head comes through, and the head of the animal hangs upon his chest. A garter made of skunk's skin with the head and tail on, shows that he has successfully taken a scalp under the enemy's fire. He wears a grizzly bear's claws when he has been surrounded, but charged singly, bear-like, and repulsed the enemy. The paws of a grizzly bear, claws and all, denote that he has knocked off or pulled off the foe in a mounted encounter.

The deer-tail head-gear dyed in shades of red, with a thin square of bone, resembling ivory, in the center, to which one or more eagle feathers are attached, is equivalent to the eagle feather war-bonnet. The quill end of each feather is placed in the hollow of a goose's wing-bone embossed with the beautiful iridescent neck-skin of a drake, and the whole forms an imposing ornament.

The wearing of the skins of certain animals and birds represents the totem, or, as it were, the coat-of-arms of the Indian. These symbols take a wide range, almost every familiar bird and animal, even fish and reptiles, being used as a sort of charm or talisman, some for healing, and others for protection from harm. But these things are not mere dead feathers or skins to the Indians; they symbolize an appeal to the brotherly spirit of the animal representing their individual lodge or clan, and are honored in recognition of the wonderful intuitive power of the dumb creatures. The Indian believes that instinct comes more directly from the " Great Mystery " than reason even; why else does an animal or child show wisdom without thought?

The addition of an ermine skin to the war-bonnet is an honor that few warriors earned in the old days. It is a degree of the highest type. The man who is recognized as a past master of courage, having achieved all the decorations of a patriot and a true warrior, dauntless in war, yet gentle at home, a friend and a brother — he alone may wear ermine upon his war-bonnet, or trim his ceremonial shirt with the beautiful white fur.

The addition of buffalo-hair trimming to a warrior's bonnet or shirt or leggings is an indication that he has taken many scalps. If he is a chief, he may even have a buffalo tail dangle from one of his teepee poles. No one may do so without the authority of the tribe. Neither can the councilors confer these degrees without

actual proof of service. No favoritism
is possible under our system, and the highest degrees are conferred only upon men
who have been tried again and again by
every conceivable ordeal. Heroism is common, because the universal spirit of gal-
lantry and chivalry requires it.

At a public dance, an Indian may re-
count some particular brave deed. This
he acts out for the benefit of the younger
element. He could not add anything to
it, because the event is already well known.
When the old customs were intact, it was
the old warriors who claimed this privilege, and they, too, were allowed to paint
their bodies in imitation of their severe
wounds.

I remember very well in a great tribal
dance that there were many of these old
men who enacted their deeds with great
spirit, and one had painted the upper half
of his face black, with zig-zag lines representing lightning, the whole symbolic of
a terrific battle. The lower part of his

face, even with the mouth and including
it was painted red, with streaks running
down upon the chin. Every Indian would
know that he had been wounded in the
mouth. Another had painted in the middle of his broad chest a red hole, and from
it there ran some red streaks, with a fine
Crow arrow depicted in realistic fashion.

These customs have their barbarous
side, but a really touching feature is that
a warrior always shares his honors with
his war-horse. Such a horse may wear an
eagle plume in his forelock as proudly as
his master, his tail or mane may be trimmed
and dyed according to his rider's war record, or he may be made to mourn for him
by having it cut quite short.

Sometimes an acknowledged warrior
decorates his long pipe-stem or the handle
of his war-club. But no person can wear
the honorable insignia of another; in fact,
he can wear none that have not been
awarded to him in due course by the council of his tribe.

The Boy Scouts may, if they choose, adapt this system to the honors counted in their organization, grading the various exploits in accordance with the real manhood needed to accomplish them.

XIX

INDIAN CEREMONIES FOR BOY SCOUTS

INDIAN ceremonies are always in demand, and I shall give you several which have been specially adapted to your use from the ancient rites of the Sioux nation.

THE AY'—CHAY—TEE, OR SCOUT'S BONFIRE

This is supposed to bring success in war and hunting, and may be kindled by a band of Scouts on the eve of a long hike, or any important undertaking, or as a ceremony of initiation of new members.

The one appointed to act as Leader or Medicine-man lays in a convenient place a pile of dry wood for the ceremonial fire, to which the Scouts are summoned by a herald. He goes the rounds with a camp

horn, bidding all come to the Ay'-chay-tee
when the sun is at a certain height in the
heavens, preferably near sunset. The
Medicine-man should be attired in full
Indian costume, and prepared to act the
part of a man full of years and wisdom.
As fire is the symbol of enthusiasm, energy,
and devotion, and is with the Indians a
strictly masculine emblem, it is fit that
the young men gather about it before
going upon a journey or " war-path."

When all have assembled in the usual
circle, dressed either in Indian costume
or Scout's uniform, the Leader, standing
in the center of the ring beside the prepared wood, kindles a " new fire " by
means of the bow and drill, flint and steel,
or " rubbing sticks."

He then takes up the long-handled cal-
umet or peace-pipe, which has previously
been filled with dried sumach leaves, red
willow bark, or other aromatic herb, kindles it with a coal from the " sacred fire,"
and reverently holding it before him in

both hands, with the stem pointing upward and forward, exclaims:

" To the Great Spirit (or Great Mystery) who is over all! "

The Scouts answer in unison: " Ho! "

Then, turning the stem of the pipe downward, the Leader says:

" To our Grandmother, the Earth! "

The Scouts answer: " Ho! "

He thus holds the pipe successively toward the four points of the compass, exclaiming as he does so: " To the East Wind! the West Wind! the North Wind! the South Wind! " and each time all answer: " Ho! "

The Leader next holds the stem of the pipe toward the first Scout, who, stepping forward and touching it solemnly, repeats in an audible voice the " Scout's Oath: "

" I promise to obey my Leader, to seek honor above all things, and that neither pain nor danger shall keep me from doing my duty! "

After the pipe has thus gone round the
circle, it is laid beside the fire, and all the
Scouts chant, or recite in unison, the
Strong Heart Song:

" We are the Scouts of —— (name of band or bri-
    gade);
We are the strong-hearted;
We go forward, fearing nothing, to fulfil our vow! "

All now dance around the fire, going
through the actions of a Scout on the
enemy's trail. A drum beaten in quick
time is the proper accompaniment to this
dance, or it may be performed to the
chant and hand-clapping of the Leader.
(For other songs and musical airs, see
Alice Fletcher's " Indian Story and Song.")
Finally the Scouts leave the ring one by
one, each, as he disappears in the shadows,
giving the yelp of the wolf — the Indian
Scout's call.

When a Scout returns to camp with
news, he is met by the councilors seated
in a circle about the fire, and before giving

his report, takes the oath of the pipe in the past tense, thus:

" I have obeyed my Leader, have sought honor above all things, and neither pain nor danger has kept me from doing my duty! "

If, however, the matter is urgent, and there is little time for ceremony, he may, on entering the circle, kick down and scatter a small pile of wood which has been placed in readiness, this act constituting his oath that he has faithfully performed his task.

THE BEAR DANCE

This is one of a class of ceremonies common among Indians, in which the actors masquerade as animals. Bears, wolves, buffalo, elk, and others are represented with elaborate costuming and imagery. The Bear is the emblem of courage.

In this dance one of the players is chosen to represent the Bear, and should be made up if possible with the skin and head of that animal as a disguise, otherwise with a painted mask. A small arbor of green boughs forms the den, from which he issues from time to time in short rushes, growling as savagely as possible, and is teased with switches in the hands of the other players. If any one can touch the Bear without being himself touched, he scores one point, but if touched, he loses five points. If he trips and falls while running, he is out of the game. Whenever the pace becomes too swift for him, the Bear may retreat to his den, where he is safe. This game should last a given number of minutes, say twenty, at the end of which the scores are reckoned by two tellers previously detailed, and the winner announced. The drum and Indian songs may accompany this entertainment, which should be followed by a feast of Indian dishes, such as corn, venison, maple sugar, etc., served in Indian style, all the guests being seated cross-legged in a circle.

THE PEACE CEREMONY

This is a very old rite of the Sioux, intended to typify the conquest of the Thunder-Bird, which is supposed to bring the lightning, and is the emblem of destruction. It is appropriately given in early summer, the period of frequent thunderstorms.

Cut the figure of the Thunder-Bird

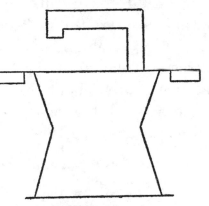

Fig. 19.

from a piece of birch-bark or thin wood, and suspend from the top of a pole fifteen feet high, which is raised in the center of a ring sixty feet in diameter, formed of small bent saplings or willow wands. The ring must have two entrances. At the foot of the pole, place a bowl of clear water to represent the rain which accompanies

the lightning. On either side stand two
small boys, dressed in red or wearing red
about their clothing, and carrying war-
clubs in their hands. These boys represent War.

Now all the Scouts enter the ring in
single file, dressed in Scouts' uniform or
Indian costume and armed with bow and
arrows. The drum beats a slow tattoo
as they march about the pole, looking upward toward the figure of the Thunder-
Bird and chanting these lines:

> " Hear us, O Thunder!
> Hear us, and tremble!
> We are the soldiers,
> Soldiers of peace! "

At the close of the song, each in turn
shoots an arrow at the image, and when
it falls, the Scout who brought it down
must drink all the water in the bowl. The
war-clubs are then taken away from the
two little boys representing War, who go
out by the western entrance to the ring.
At the same time there enter by the east-

ern entrance two more boys (or preferably girls, if it is a mixed assemblage), clad in blue and carrying calumets, to typify Peace. These lead the second march around the pole, while all chant the second stanza of the song:

" The Thunder is fallen;
Lost are his arrows;
Peace is the victor —
Our mother is Peace! "

A heavy stick with a large knot or knob on the end will do for a war-club, and if no genuine peace-pipe is obtainable, one may be improvised from a piece of wood.

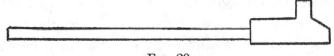

FIG. 20.

To any or all of these ceremonies spectators may be invited (and among the Indians the whole village is generally present), but it is essential that they maintain perfect order and absolute silence during the solemnities.

XX

THE MAIDENS' FEAST: A CEREMONY FOR GIRLS

A BEAUTIFUL festival, celebrated
yearly in the olden time among the
Sioux and other Plains Indians, was
called the " Maidens' Feast," and was designed to stimulate a proper pride and
dedication to duty among the young girls
of the tribe. I shall describe for you an
adaptation of this ancient ceremony, that
may be appropriately used by Camp Fire
Girls and others on their summer outings.

This feast is always given at midsummer,
in the fullness of bloom and splendor, as
befits a gathering of the flower of the village or community. Invitations may be
issued by the Guardian of the Camp Fire,
or Leader of the band of girls, in the
form of thin leaves of birch-bark or small
bunches of sweet-grass. Another way of

giving the invitation, if all the girls are in
camp, is to engage the services of some
man with a bugle or camp-horn to act as
herald. He should dress in Indian costume and make the rounds early in the
morning, blowing the horn and declaim-
ing in a loud voice somewhat as follows:

" Hear ye, hear ye, all the people! The
maidens of the . . . Camp Fire are summoned to repair at noon to-day to the Sacred Stone in the middle of the encamp-
ment, there to hold the annual feast! Hear
ye, hear ye! "

The maidens all come in ceremonial
attire, and full Indian costume is indis-
pensable to the proper effect. The hair is
arranged in forward-turning plaits, and
surmounted by a modest wreath or fillet
of wild flowers. They advance silently,
in single file, and form a ring about the
" Sacred Stone," a rudely heart-shaped
or pyramidal boulder, which has been
touched lightly with red paint. Beside
the Stone, two new arrows are thrust into

the earth. The rock symbolizes permanence, or the unchangeable forces of nature; the arrows, nature's punishment for disobedience.

Now the leader of the maidens steps out of the ring, and laying her right hand upon the summit of the Stone, pronounces in clear tones the " Maidens' Vow: "

" Upon this Stone I take the maiden's twofold vow; the vow of purity — my duty to myself; the pledge of service — my duty to others! "

She then steps back and seats herself sidewise on the ground in the ring. Each in turn takes the vow in the same manner until the " maidens' circle " is complete. Then all rise and chant, or recite in unison, the " Maidens' Song: "

" We are the maidens of —— (name of band);
Our faces are turned toward the morning;
In our hearts is the summer of promise;
In our hands " (make cup of both hands) " we hold
    the new generation!
United we go to meet the future,
Armed with truth to ourselves, and with love for
    all! "

At the close of the song, all take hands
and dance four times about the Stone,
each time reversing the movement.

Lastly, they seat themselves again in
the same order, and the " feast " is served
by handing it about the circle, each maiden
taking her portion in her own basin, or
bowl, and eating it with her own spoon,
having brought these with her according
to the Indian custom.   Appropriate dishes
for the feast would be rice with maple
sugar (wild rice if obtainable), green corn
or succotash, berries and nuts, maize
cakes or pop-corn dainties, or any strictly
native product.   After the food is served,
it is permitted for the first time to talk and
laugh, all gravity and decorum having been
preserved by participants and spectators
during the entire ceremony.

The parents and friends of the young
women should be invited, if convenient,
to witness the " Maidens' Feast," and a
characteristic Indian feature would be
added if some of them should desire to

signalize the occasion by gifts to some needy person or cause. Such gifts should be announced at the close of the festival.

XXI

THE GESTURE - LANGUAGE OF THE INDIAN

THE American Indian is extremely pictorial in his habits of thought and in his modes of expression. Even his every-day speech is full of symbols drawn from the natural world. Yet more poetic and descriptive in character is that form of communication properly called "gesture speech," but commonly known as "Indian sign-language."

This language is most fully developed among the tribes of the Great Plains, many of whom speak entirely different tongues, for use in their frequent meetings, either accidental or for the purpose of concluding a treaty of peace. It is also used by deaf mutes among Indians. It has been learned and elaborately written out by several au-

thorities, chief of whom is Captain W. R.
Clark of the United States Army. Being
understood by few, it will serve excellently
as a secret code, so much desired by young
people, and is especially appropriate to the
ceremonials of Boy Scouts and Camp Fire
Girls.

We Indian boys were taught from babyhood to be silent, to listen to the things
that nature is saying all about us. But
since it is hard for a healthy boy to keep
his discoveries and observations entirely to
himself, he must devise some outlet. Our
silent communication, our " wireless," was
the gesture-language.

It should be remembered that among
Indians the whole body speaks, and that all
oratory, and even conversation, is accompanied by graceful and significant gestures.
The accomplished user will make the signs
herein described rapidly and smoothly, in-
vesting the whole with genuine charm, as
a novel kind of pantomime. For it will
be seen that these are no arbitrary signs,

but actual air-pictures, and not manual only, since they include a variety of movements and considerable facial expression.

The construction or grammar of the sign-language is simple. Adjectives follow nouns, conjunctions and prepositions are omitted, and verbs are used in the present tense only. The following signs, well-learned, will enable one to carry on a short conversation, and many more may be devised along these lines by an ingenious boy or girl.

Attention, or Question. Hold right hand, palm outward, fingers and thumb separated, well out in front of body at height of shoulder. This is used to begin a conversation.

I understand. Throw right forearm out in front of body with fingers closed, except index finger, which is curved and drawn back. This indicates that you grasp and draw something toward you, and is used occasionally while another is talking. If you do not understand, use the *Question* sign.

I. Touch breast with index finger of right hand.

Glad. (Sunshine in the heart.) Place compressed right hand, fingers slightly curved, over region of heart; bring left hand, palm downward, in sweeping curve to left of body, at the same time turning it palm upward, as if turning up or unfolding something. The expression of the face should correspond.

Sad. Place the closed fist against the heart. Appropriate facial expression.

Surprised. Cover mouth with palm of right hand, open eyes widely, and move head slightly backward.

Angry. (Mind twisted.) Place closed right fist against forehead and twist from right to left.

Ashamed. (Blanket over face.) Bring both hands, palms inward, fingers touching, in front of and near the face.

Good. (Level with heart.) Hold extended right hand, back up, close to region of heart; move briskly forward and to right.

Bad. (Throw away.) Hold one or both hands, closed, in front of body, backs upward; open with a snap, at the same time moving them outward and downward.

Brave, Strong. Hold firmly closed left hand in front of body, left arm pointing to right and front; bring closed right hand above and a little in front of left, and strike downwards, imitating the blow of a hammer. (This gesture, vigorously made, intensifies any previous statement or description.)

Alone. Hold up index finger.

On Horseback. Place first and second finger of right hand astride left index finger. Motion of galloping may be made, or a *Fall* from the horse represented.

Tent, or Wigwam. Bring both hands together at the finger tips, forming a cone.

House. Interlock fingers of both hands, holding them at right angles.

Camp. Sign for *Tent*, then form circle with arms and hands in front of body.

City, or Village. Sign for *House*, then *Camp* sign.

Sleep. Incline head to right and rest cheek on right palm. For going into camp, or to indicate the length of a journey, make sign for *Sleep* and hold up as many fingers as nights were spent on the way.

Time is told by indicating the position of the sun; the *Seasons* as follows:

Spring. (Little grass.) Hold hands, palms upward, well down in front, fingers and thumbs well separated and slightly curved; separate hands slightly. Then hold right hand in front of body, back to right, closing fingers so that only tip of index finger projects. (This last sign for *Little.*)

Summer. Sign for *Grass*, holding hands at height of waist.

Autumn. (Falling leaves.) Hold right hand above head, fingers closed, except index finger and thumb, which form nearly a circle; bring hand slowly downward with wavering motion.

Winter. Hold closed hands in front of body and several inches apart; give shivering motion to hands.

To indicate *Age*, give sign for *Winter* and hold up fingers; all counting is done in the same way, in multiples of ten; as, for one hundred, open and close fingers of both hands ten times.

Color is usually indicated by pointing to some object of the color spoken of.

Brother. Touch first and second finger to lips.

Sister. Sign for *Brother*, and that for *Woman.*

Woman. (Long hair.) Bring both palms down sides of head, shoulders, and bosom, with sweeping gesture.

Love. Cross both arms over bosom.

Give Me. Hold right hand well out in front of body, palm upward, close, and bring in toward body.

Beautiful. Hold palms up like mirror in front of face; make sign for *Good.*

Ugly. Same as above, with sign for *Bad.*

Peace. Clasp both hands in front of body.

Quarrel. Hold index fingers, pointing upward, opposite and a few inches apart; move sharply toward each other, alternating motion.

Liar. (Forked tongue.) Bring separated first and second fingers of right hand close to lips.

Scout. (This is also the sign for *Wolf*.) Hold first and second fingers of right hand, extended and pointing upward, near right shoulder, to indicate pointed ears.

Trail. Hold extended hands, palms up, side by side in front of body; move right to rear and left to front a few inches; alternate motion.

It is finished. Bring closed hands in front of body, thumbs up, second joints touching; then separate. This sign ends a speech or conversation.

XXII

INDIAN PICTURE-WRITING

THE Indian is something of an impressionist in the matter of technique. Though possessed of great manual dexterity, he does not care, as a rule, to reproduce an object exactly, but rather to suggest his fundamental conception of it. Each drawing stands for an idea, and its symbolic character gives it a certain mystery and dignity in our eyes.

It is usual to represent an animal in action, in order to indicate more clearly its real or imaginary attributes. Thus a horse is shown running, a buffalo or bear fighting, or in a humorous attitude.

Pictorial hieroglyphics are merely crude pictures drawn and painted upon leather or birch-bark, or cut into the trunk of a

convenient tree, or perhaps upon a hard
clay bank, and sometimes even scratched
with a hard stone upon the face of a cliff.
In the first place, they represent history
and biography, and serve to supplement
and authenticate our oral traditions.
Others are communications intended for
some one who is likely to pass that way,
and give important information. The per-

FIG. 21.

son or persons whom it is desired to reach
need not be addressed, but the sender of
the message signs his name first, as in a letter
of ceremony.

Suppose Charging Eagle is on the war-
path and wishes to communicate with his
friends. He cuts· upon the bark of a conspicuous tree beside the trail the figure of
an eagle swooping downward, bearing in

its beak a war-club. The news he gives is that his young men brought home a herd of horses taken from the enemy. He draws first a teepee; facing it are several free horses, and immediately behind them two or three riders with war-bonnets on their heads, leading another horse. Last of all are some horses' footprints. The free horses represent force, and the led horse expresses captivity. The fact that the men wear their war-bonnets, indicates a state of war.

The event is dated by drawing the symbol of the month in which it occurred, followed by the outline of the moon in its first, second, third, or fourth quarter, dark or full, as the case may be. The waxing moon opens toward the right, the waning moon toward the left. To be still more exact, the chief may draw the sun with its rays, followed by an open hand with as many fingers extended as days have passed since the event.

The thirteen moons of the year are

named differently by different Indian tribes.
I will give the names and symbols com-

Fig. 22

monly used by the Sioux, beginning with
nature's new year, the early spring.

1. Ish-tah'-wee-chah'- Moon of Sore Eyes.
   ya-zan-wee.
2. Mah-gah'-o-kah'- Moon of Ducks' Eggs.
   dah-wee.
3. Wah-to'-pah-wee. Canoeing Moon.
4. Wee'-pah-zoo-kah- June-Berry Moon.
   wee.
5. Wah-shoon'-pah- Moon of Moulting Feath-
   wee.   ers.
6. Chan-pah-sap'-ah- Moon of Black Cherries.
   wee.
7. Psin-ah'-tee-wee. Wild-Rice Gathering Moon.
8. Wah-soo'-ton-wee'. Moon of Green Corn.
9. Wok'-sah-pee-wee'. Moon of Corn Harvest.

10. Tah-kee'-yoo-hah'-   Moon of Mating Deer.
    wee'.
11. Tah-hay'-chap-   Moon of Dropping Deer-
    shoon'-wee.   horns.
12. Wee-tay'-ghee.   Moon of Severe Cold.
13. We-chah'-tah-wee.   Raccoon's Moon

In the old days, there were many different bands of the Sioux, who wandered,
during the year, over a wide extent of country. Thus news was spread both by signal
communication and by pictographs, when
it was impossible to communicate by word
of mouth. This particular message of
Charging Eagle's was not only news, but
also a warning to travelers to be on their
guard, for the enemy might seek to re-
taliate, and some innocent persons be surprised and made to pay dearly for another's
exploit.

In picture-writing, the head of man or
animal is emphasized, with its distinguishing
peculiarity of head-gear, or ears, or horns,
while the body is barely outlined. The
warrior is represented by a rude figure of
a man wearing a war-bonnet, or carrying

a coup-staff. Warriors returning successful
are shown approaching a group of teepees,
carrying scalps on poles. If, on the con-

Fig. 23.

trary, the writer's camp has been raided,
the figures are seen departing from the teepees. A trail, or journey, is indicated by
double wavy lines. If the travelers parted,
the trail is branched.

Fig. 24.

Lightning is represented by zigzag lines
with a suggestion of flames at the points,
or by a large bird with zigzag flashes
issuing from his beak. Wind is indicated

by tossed clouds; but for the four winds, or four points of the compass, draw a mere cross, or a pair of crossed arrows. For rain, make dots and dashes; for snow, falling stars; for night, stars above a black line, sometimes adding a crescent moon.

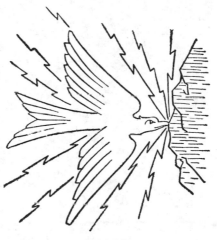

FIG. 25.

Every Indian has his pictographic signature, and this idea may appropriately be copied by Boy Scouts, who will also enjoy communicating by Indian signs and keeping the record book or "winter count" in the same manner.

The name "Sitting Bull," for example, is drawn as a buffalo bull sitting upon its haunches, with front feet in the air and tossing head. Spotted Tail is a charger with luxuriant flowing tail, streaked and spotted with white. Hawk Eagle signs his name by drawing a hawk wearing an eagle feather war-bonnet. Big Tent draws a large teepee, with a buffalo tail dangling from the pro-jecting poles, to show dig-nity and im-portance. The autograph of Chief Bullhead is the figure of a man with the

FIG. 26.

head of a bull buffalo, perhaps surmounted by a war-bonnet.

The " ghost," or spirit, is represented by a pair of eyes looking from the sky, or by the outline of a bird with great eyes. Prayer, or the " Great Mystery," is sym-bolized by the figure of a man in the In-dian's prayer attitude — standing erect,

with head uplifted and the tips of his
fingers meeting in a sharp angle in front
of his chest, gazing at the figure of the
sun.

XXIII

WOOD - CRAFT AND WEATHER WISDOM

SINCE the life of the Indian is one of travel and exploration, not for the benefit of science, but for his own convenience and pleasure, he is accustomed to find himself in pathless regions — now in the deep woods, now upon the vast, shimmering prairie, or again among the tangled water-ways of a mighty lake studded with hundreds, even thousands, of wooded islands.

How does he find his way so successfully in the pathless jungle without the aid of a compass? you ask. Well, it is no secret. In the first place, his vision is correct; and he is not merely conscious of what he sees, but also sub-consciously he observes the presence of any and all things within the range of his senses.

If you would learn his system, you must
note the relative position of all objects, and
especially the location of your camp in relation to river, lake, or mountain.   The
Indian is a close student of the topography
of the country, and every landmark —
hill, grove, or unusual tree — is noted and
remembered.   It is customary with the
hunters and warriors to tell their stories of
adventure most minutely, omitting no geographical and topographical details, so
that the boy who has listened to such
stories from babyhood can readily identify
places he has never before seen.

This kind of knowledge is simple, and,
like the every-day meal, it is properly di-
gested and assimilated, and becomes a part
of one's self.   It is this instant, intelligent
recognition of every object within his
vision in his daily roving, which fixes the
primitive woodsman's reckoning of time,
distance, and direction.

Time is measured simply by the height
of the sun.   Shadow is the wild man's dial;

his own shadow is best. Hunger is a good guide when the sun is behind the clouds. Again, the distance traveled is an indicator, when one travels over known distances. In other words, he keeps his soul at one with the world about him, while the over-civilized man is trained to depend upon artificial means. He winds his watch, pins his thought to a chronometer, and disconnects himself from the world-current; then starts off on the well-beaten road. If he is compelled to cut across, he calls for a guide; in other words, he borrows or buys the mind of another. Neither can he trust his memory, but must needs have a notebook!

The wild man has no chronometer, no yardstick, no unit of weight, no field-glass. He is himself a natural being in touch with nature. Some things he does, he scarcely knows why; certainly he could not explain them. His calculations are swift as a flash of lightning; best of all, they come out right! This may seem incredible to one who is

born an old man; but there are still some
boys who hark back to their great-great-
grandfathers; they were not born and
nursed within six walls!

The colors of tree, grass, and rock tell
the points of the compass to the initiated.
On the north side, the bark is of a darker
color, smoother, and more solid looking;
while on the southern exposure it is of a
lighter hue, because of more sunshine, and
rougher, because it has not been polished
off by the heavy beating of snow and rain
in the cold season. An Indian will pass
his hand over the trunk of a tree in the
dark and tell you which way is north; some
will tell you the kind of tree, also.

The branches of the tree tell the same
story; on the south side they grow thicker
and longer, while the leaves lie more horizontal on the sunny side, and more vertical
on the north. Again, the dry leaves on the
ground corroborate them; on the north
side of the trees the leaves are well-packed
and overlay each other almost like shingles.

The color and thickness of the moss on rock or tree also tells the secret.

But I must leave some things for you to discover; and I advise you to select a rock or tree that is well exposed to the elements for a first attempt. Of course, in well-protected localities, these distinctions are not so marked, but even there are discernible to a trained eye.

If you ever lose your way in the woods, do not allow yourself to become unnerved. Never " give up." Fear drowns more people than water, and is a more dangerous enemy than the wilderness. A normal man, with some knowledge of out-of-doors, can without much effort keep in touch with his starting-point, and, however tortuously he may rove, he will pick the shortest way back. Know exactly where you are before starting, in relation to the natural landmarks, and at every halt locate yourself as nearly as possible. Measure your shadow (it varies according to the season), and scatter dry earth, leaves, or grass, to

learn the direction of the wind. The water-
shed is another important point to bear in
mind. On a clear night, look for the well-
known stars, such as the " Great Dipper,"
which lies to the north in summer, the
handle pointing west. The " Milky Way "
lies north and south. Once you locate the
camp, you may be guided by these or by
the wind in night travel.

The Indian, as an out-of-door man,
early learns the necessity of a weather
bureau of his own. He develops it after
the fashion of another system of precaution;
that is, he takes note of the danger-signals
of the animals, those unconscious criers of
the wilderness, both upon water and land.
These have definite signals for an approaching change in the weather. For instance,
the wolf tribes give the "storm call" on
the evening before. This call is different
in tone from any other and clearly identified
by us. Horses kick and stamp, and the
buffalo herds low nervously. Certain water-
fowl display a strange agitation which

they do not show under any other circumstances. Antelopes seek shallow lakes before a thunder-shower and stand in the water — the Indians say because lightning does not strike in the water. Even dogs howl and make preparations to hide their young. Ducks have their signal call; but the chief weather prophet of the lakes is the loon, as the gray wolf or coyote is of the prairie.

Certain leaves and grass-blades contract or expand at the approach of storm, and even their color is affected, while the wind in the leaves has a different sound. The waves on the beach whisper of the change, and we also observe the " ring " around the sun, and the opacity and disk of the moon. The lone hunter may be left with only the open prairie and the dome of heaven; but he still has his grass-blades, his morning and evening skies. Sometimes the little prairie birds give him the signal; or, if not, he may fall back upon his old wounds, that begin to ache and swell with the change of atmosphere.

XXIV

THE ART OF STORY-TELLING

PERHAPS no other people enjoy good stories better, and are more apt at telling them, than are the Indians. This art, most highly prized in a race without books, serves as a necessary outlet to their imaginations, and wonderfully enlivens their social and family life. The time for telling Indian stories is in the evening — best of all, around a glowing wood fire, on the long nights of winter. Here, every accent, every gesture, has its meaning, no faintest shade of which is lost upon the circle of attentive listeners.

True stories of warfare and the chase are related many times over by actors and eyewitnesses, that no detail may be forgotten. Handed down from generation to generation, these tales gradually take on the proportions of heroic myth and legend. They blossom into poetry and chivalry, and are alive with mystery and magic. The pictures are vivid, and drawn with few but masterly strokes. Often animals as well as men are the villains and heroes, and in this way a grotesque humor is artfully yet naturally developed.

In the old days, it was customary among us for each clan to have its official story-teller, whose skill in making the most of his material had built up a reputation which might extend even to neighboring villages. He was not only an entertainer in demand at all social gatherings, but an honored schoolmaster to the village children. The great secret of his success was his ability to portray a character or a situation truth-fully, yet with just a touch of humorous or dramatic exaggeration. The scene is clearly visualized; the action moves quickly, with successive events leading up to the climax, which must be handled with much dignity and seriousness, or pathos and gravity may be turned upside down in the unexpectedness of the catastrophe.

Here is a short example of Indian story-telling:

Far out in the middle of the "Bad Lands," upon the Little Missouri, there stands a pillar-like butte some four or five hundred paces in height. Here and there upon its sheer walls cling a few stunted pines and cedars, some hanging by one foot, others by their great toe only. Not one of the many gulches that furrow its sides affords a safe path, or even a tolerable ladder to the top. There is generally a pair of eagles who breed there, and an occasional Rocky Mountain sheep may be seen springing along its terraces. We Indians have long regarded this butte as a sacred temple, the very spot for solitary prayer and fasting; but tradition states that only two men have ever set foot upon its summit for this purpose.

Feared-by-the-Bear was a warrior of unquestioned bravery. One day he announced that he would fast upon Cloud Butte. Thereupon other well-known braves decided to fast there also. Their leader managed the ascent with much labor and difficulty. When, just at sunset, he reached the summit, he was happy; the world seemed revealed to him in all its beauty and majesty. "Where can such another shrine be found?" he thought.

He took his position upon a narrow projection of rock extending over the abyss, where it is said no human being has stood before or since. The full moon had risen, and the brave stood above that silvered gulf of air with uplifted filled pipe and extended arm, praying without words, as is our custom.

Suddenly his ears rang with the cry: "Haya háy! A grizzly! A grizzly!" He was compelled to suspend his devotions for an instant, and to throw a glance in the direction of the call. He perceived that his example had been followed, and that what seemed an avenging spirit was pursuing his fellow worshipper.

"Dodge behind a tree! Run your best; he is almost upon you!" he shouted. But the nearest tree hung upon the verge of the precipice. If the man missed his footing, he must go down to death.

There was no time to consider. Around the tree he flew and disappeared like a passing shadow. At his heels the desperate grizzly, who had prolonged his unwilling fast upon the butte for days, not daring to attempt the descent, lunged heavily against the swaying cedar to save himself from falling headlong. He was half a second too late!

Feared-by-the-Bear had not yet been discovered. He clutched his long pipe and still pointed it toward the starry sky in silent supplication. Indeed, he had now more immediate cause for prayer. "Waugh!" uttered the hungry bear, and approached him with wide-open mouth.

The dizzy shelf on which the brave

stood had been an eagle's nest for ages, but was just now unoccupied. Old Mato, the bear, seemed reluctant to advance, for on either side the sheer rock descended to a great distance. The warrior merely turned toward him the filled pipe which he had been offering to the "Great Mystery."

"To your spirit, O Bear! I offer this peace pipe, the same I have just offered to the Maker of us both. Will you partake of it, and commission me to be as brave and strong as yourself?" Thus speaking, and without showing any nervousness, he pointed the long stem of the pipe directly at the bear, upon which Mato growled ungraciously, but did not offer to come nearer. On the other hand, he showed no intention of leaving, and the way to escape was blocked.

Feared-by-the-Bear lighted his pipe with the "fire maker," and smoked deliberately. Then he kindled a little fire in the dry twigs of the old eagle's nest. This seemed to disturb the bear, whereupon he boldly

threw a firebrand at him. The dry leaves
caught and blazed fiercely. Mato ran for
his life, and with this new fright behind
him, found no serious difficulty in getting
down the trail.

In due time, the faster left his position
with all dignity, and approached the lean-
ing cedar tree behind which his friend, as
he supposed, had leaped to death. His
first shuddering look over the brink showed
him that the young man still hung suspended by his hands from a large branch.
With much difficulty he was dragged up to
solid rock, and his involuntary ordeal
brought to a close. This event established
the names and reputations of " Overcliff "
and " Feared-by-the-Bear."

XXV

ETIQUETTE OF THE WIGWAM

THE natural life of the Indian is saved from rudeness and disorder by certain well-understood rules and conventions which are invariably followed. Simple as these rules may seem, they have stood the test of time, and are universally respected. You may be able to adapt some of them to the government of your camp.

Each band has its chief, or leader, who governs through his council, and a herald to announce their decisions. Scouts and soldiers are appointed by the council. When several bands camp together, all know that there will be no change in the general order, aside from a few special and temporary rules. The clans simply enforce the usual codes conjointly, though any special service necessarily carries with it greater honor, because of serving a larger community.

If a member of any band commits an offence against one of another band, all the chiefs constitute the grand jury. Their verdict is attested by the grand council, while the two persons affected have no voice in the matter, except as they may be called upon to testify of what they know. The punishment decreed is strictly carried out without prejudice or favoritism. No boy or man can flee from the voice and hand of justice. Where can he go and be at peace with his own conscience?

I have said elsewhere that the tents are pitched in a circle, or group of circles. In case of a large band, their position in the circle is determined by their relative strength and reputation. The strongest band takes its place on the right of the entrance, and the next strongest takes the left. Opposite the entrance is the post of honor, which is accorded to the greatest chief or temporary head of the large camp.

Now the family circle in the wigwam is arranged on the same principle. The circle is symbolic of life, also symbolic of the day's journey. Woman rules the lodge; therefore on the right of the entrance is the position of the grandmother, if there is one. Next her are her granddaughters, the youngest nearest her. Then comes the grandfather, and next him the grown sons, if any; then the father, and between him and the mother, who occupies the first seat on the left of the entrance, are one or two of the smallest children. The guest is seated opposite the entrance.

It is a rule of the Indian home that the grandfather is master of ceremonies at all times. He is spokesman for the family if a stranger enters. If he is absent, the father or the husband speaks; all others may only smile in greeting. If both men are absent, the grandmother is spokeswoman; if she is away, the mother or the

wife speaks, with as much dignity as
modesty. If no older person is at home,
the eldest son or daughter greets the guest,
but if they have no brother to speak for
them, and an entire stranger enters, the
girls may properly observe silence. The
stranger should explain the cause of his
intrusion.

In the presence of a guest, promiscuous
laughing or a careless attitude are not permitted. Rigid decorum and respectful
silence are observed, and if any children
are present, they must not stare at the
stranger. All noisy play and merriment
must be kept within familiar family circles,
except on the occasion of certain games
and dances.

In the matter of greetings, the men alone
greet each other with " How! " No woman
may use this greeting. Indians do not usually say " Thank you! " but acknowl-
edge a gift or favor by using some appropriate term of relationship, as grandmother,
little sister, cousin, etc. " Hi, hi! " or

" Thank you! " is occasionally used, but only when one is especially grateful.

You should always address everybody in the clan by the regular term of relationship, rather than by name. If too distant, the word " Kólah," or friend, may be used. Perhaps a prettier word for the Boy Scouts to adopt is " Kechúwah," or comrade.

The serving of food is always orderly and polite. Guests are offered food, at whatever hour of the day they may appear, as, in the wilderness life, it is safe to assume that they are hungry. The mother of the family serves first the guest, if any, then her father, her husband, her mother, the children in order of age, and, of course, herself last of all. Each returns his empty dish to her with the proper term of relationship as a sign of thanks.

Silence, we believe, is the basis of order and decorum, and the peace and dignity of the camp must be maintained at all costs. Thus any emergency is quickly made known and is met with calmness and decision. All formal announcements are made by the mouth of the camp herald or crier.

Our Indian " Boy Scouts " are the immediate and unofficial guardians of our safety. If any one approaches, they quickly pass the unspoken signal from boy to boy, without letting the stranger know that he is discovered; and if there is any doubt as to his identity and character, that, too, is indicated, so that the experienced may see to it before he comes too near. The reports of the returning hunters are given by means of certain calls, so that the home folks may be prepared to receive them.

For instance, when a bear is killed, the boys announce it with the peculiar call, " Wah, wah, wah! " in chorus. If it is a deer, they cry: " Woo koo hoo'! woo koo hoo'! " In welcoming the buffalo hunters, the boys hold one another by the shoulders and imitate the lowing of the herds, finishing off with a shrill whistle. Possibly your college and class yells were founded upon the Indian game signals.

XXVI

TRAINING FOR SERVICE

ONE must have a trained mind, if only in order to reach the height of one's physical possibilities, and all-round efficiency depends much upon the kind of training described in the foregoing talks. The " School of Savagery " is no haphazard thing, but a system of education which has been long in the building, and which produces results. Ingenuity, faithfulness, and self-reliance will accomplish wonderful things in civilized life as well as in wild life, but, to my mind, individuality and initiative are more successfully developed in the out-of-door man. Where the other man is regarded more than self, duty is sweeter and more inspiring, patriotism more sacred, and friendship is a true and eternal bond.

The Indian is trained in the natural
way, which means that he is kept in close
contact with the natural world. Incidentally, he finds himself, and is conscious
of his relation to all life. The spiritual
world is real to him. The splendor of life
stands out pre-eminently, while beyond
all, and in all, dwells the Great Mystery,
unsolved and unsolvable, except in those
things which it is good for his own spirit
to know.

The good things of earth are not his to
hold against his brothers, but they are his
to use and enjoy together with his fellows,
to whom it is his privilege to bring them.
In seeking thus, he develops a wholesome,
vigorous body and mind, to which all ex-
ertion seems play, rather than painful
toil for possession's sake. Happy, rollicking,
boy man! Gallant, patriotic, public-spirited
— in the Indian is the lusty youth of human-
ity. He is always ready to undertake the
impossible, or to impoverish himself to
please his friend.

Most of all he values the opportunity of being a minute-man — a Scout! Every boy, from the very beginning of his training, is an embryo public servant. He puts into daily practice the lessons that in this way become part of himself. There are no salaries, no " tips," no prizes to work for. He takes his pay in the recognition of the community and the consciousness of unselfish service. Let us have more of this spirit of the American Indian, the Boy Scout's prototype, to leaven the brilliant selfishness of our modern civilization!

THE END

A CATALOG OF SELECTED
DOVER BOOKS
IN ALL FIELDS OF INTEREST

A CATALOG OF SELECTED DOVER
BOOKS IN ALL FIELDS OF INTEREST

DRAWINGS OF REMBRANDT, edited by Seymour Slive. Updated Lippmann, Hofstede de Groot edition, with definitive scholarly apparatus. All portraits, biblical sketches, landscapes, nudes. Oriental figures, classical studies, together with selection of work by followers. 550 illustrations. Total of 630pp. 9⅛ × 12¼.
21485-0, 21486-9 Pa., Two-vol. set $25.00

GHOST AND HORROR STORIES OF AMBROSE BIERCE, Ambrose Bierce. 24 tales vividly imagined, strangely prophetic, and decades ahead of their time in technical skill: "The Damned Thing," "An Inhabitant of Carcosa," "The Eyes of the Panther," "Moxon's Master," and 20 more. 199pp. 5⅜ × 8½. 20767-6 Pa. $3.95

ETHICAL WRITINGS OF MAIMONIDES, Maimonides. Most significant ethical works of great medieval sage, newly translated for utmost precision, readability. Laws Concerning Character Traits, Eight Chapters, more. 192pp. 5⅜ × 8½.
24522-5 Pa. $4.50

THE EXPLORATION OF THE COLORADO RIVER AND ITS CANYONS, J. W. Powell. Full text of Powell's 1,000-mile expedition down the fabled Colorado in 1869. Superb account of terrain, geology, vegetation, Indians, famine, mutiny, treacherous rapids, mighty canyons, during exploration of last unknown part of continental U.S. 400pp. 5⅜ × 8½. 20094-9 Pa. $6.95

HISTORY OF PHILOSOPHY, Julián Marías. Clearest one-volume history on the market. Every major philosopher and dozens of others, to Existentialism and later. 505pp. 5⅜ × 8½. 21739-6 Pa. $8.50

ALL ABOUT LIGHTNING, Martin A. Uman. Highly readable non-technical survey of nature and causes of lightning, thunderstorms, ball lightning, St. Elmo's Fire, much more. Illustrated. 192pp. 5⅜ × 8½. 25237-X Pa. $5.95

SAILING ALONE AROUND THE WORLD, Captain Joshua Slocum. First man to sail around the world, alone, in small boat. One of great feats of seamanship told in delightful manner. 67 illustrations. 294pp. 5⅜ × 8½. 20326-3 Pa. $4.50

LETTERS AND NOTES ON THE MANNERS, CUSTOMS AND CONDITIONS OF THE NORTH AMERICAN INDIANS, George Catlin. Classic account of life among Plains Indians: ceremonies, hunt, warfare, etc. 312 plates. 572pp. of text. 6⅛ × 9¼. 22118-0, 22119-9 Pa. Two-vol. set $15.90

ALASKA: The Harriman Expedition, 1899, John Burroughs, John Muir, et al. Informative, engrossing accounts of two-month, 9,000-mile expedition. Native peoples, wildlife, forests, geography, salmon industry, glaciers, more. Profusely illustrated. 240 black-and-white line drawings. 124 black-and-white photographs. 3 maps. Index. 576pp. 5⅜ × 8½. 25109-8 Pa. $11.95

THE BOOK OF BEASTS: Being a Translation from a Latin Bestiary of the Twelfth Century, T. H. White. Wonderful catalog real and fanciful beasts: manticore, griffin, phoenix, amphivius, jaculus, many more. White's witty erudite commentary on scientific, historical aspects. Fascinating glimpse of medieval mind. Illustrated. 296pp. 5⅜ × 8¼. (Available in U.S. only) 24609-4 Pa. $5.95

FRANK LLOYD WRIGHT: ARCHITECTURE AND NATURE With 160 Illustrations, Donald Hoffmann. Profusely illustrated study of influence of nature—especially prairie—on Wright's designs for Fallingwater, Robie House, Guggenheim Museum, other masterpieces. 96pp. 9¼ × 10¾. 25098-9 Pa. $7.95

FRANK LLOYD WRIGHT'S FALLINGWATER, Donald Hoffmann. Wright's famous waterfall house: planning and construction of organic idea. History of site, owners, Wright's personal involvement. Photographs of various stages of building. Preface by Edgar Kaufmann, Jr. 100 illustrations. 112pp. 9¼ × 10. 23671-4 Pa. $7.95

YEARS WITH FRANK LLOYD WRIGHT: Apprentice to Genius, Edgar Tafel. Insightful memoir by a former apprentice presents a revealing portrait of Wright the man, the inspired teacher, the greatest American architect. 372 black-and-white illustrations. Preface. Index. vi + 228pp. 8¼ × 11. 24801-1 Pa. $9.95

THE STORY OF KING ARTHUR AND HIS KNIGHTS, Howard Pyle. Enchanting version of King Arthur fable has delighted generations with imaginative narratives of exciting adventures and unforgettable illustrations by the author. 41 illustrations. xviii + 313pp. 6⅛ × 9¼. 21445-1 Pa. $5.95

THE GODS OF THE EGYPTIANS, E. A. Wallis Budge. Thorough coverage of numerous gods of ancient Egypt by foremost Egyptologist. Information on evolution of cults, rites and gods; the cult of Osiris; the Book of the Dead and its rites; the sacred animals and birds; Heaven and Hell; and more. 956pp. 6⅛ × 9¼. 22055-9, 22056-7 Pa., Two-vol. set $20.00

A THEOLOGICO-POLITICAL TREATISE, Benedict Spinoza. Also contains unfinished Political Treatise. Great classic on religious liberty, theory of government on common consent. R. Elwes translation. Total of 421pp. 5⅜ × 8½. 20249-6 Pa. $6.95

INCIDENTS OF TRAVEL IN CENTRAL AMERICA, CHIAPAS, AND YUCATAN, John L. Stephens. Almost single-handed discovery of Maya culture; exploration of ruined cities, monuments, temples; customs of Indians. 115 drawings. 892pp. 5⅜ × 8½. 22404-X, 22405-8 Pa., Two-vol. set $15.90

LOS CAPRICHOS, Francisco Goya. 80 plates of wild, grotesque monsters and caricatures. Prado manuscript included. 183pp. 6⅛ × 9⅜. 22384-1 Pa. $4.95

AUTOBIOGRAPHY: The Story of My Experiments with Truth, Mohandas K. Gandhi. Not hagiography, but Gandhi in his own words. Boyhood, legal studies, purification, the growth of the Satyagraha (nonviolent protest) movement. Critical, inspiring work of the man who freed India. 480pp. 5⅜ × 8½. (Available in U.S. only) 24593-4 Pa. $6.95

THE ART NOUVEAU STYLE BOOK OF ALPHONSE MUCHA: All 72 Plates from "Documents Decoratifs" in Original Color, Alphonse Mucha. Rare copyright-free design portfolio by high priest of Art Nouveau. Jewelry, wallpaper, stained glass, furniture, figure studies, plant and animal motifs, etc. Only complete one-volume edition. 80pp. 9⅜ × 12¼. 24044-4 Pa. $8.95

ANIMALS: 1,419 COPYRIGHT-FREE ILLUSTRATIONS OF MAMMALS, BIRDS, FISH, INSECTS, ETC., edited by Jim Harter. Clear wood engravings present, in extremely lifelike poses, over 1,000 species of animals. One of the most extensive pictorial sourcebooks of its kind. Captions. Index. 284pp. 9 × 12. 23766-4 Pa. $9.95

OBELISTS FLY HIGH, C. Daly King. Masterpiece of American detective fiction, long out of print, involves murder on a 1935 transcontinental flight—"a very thrilling story"—NY Times. Unabridged and unaltered republication of the edition published by William Collins Sons & Co. Ltd., London, 1935. 288pp. 5⅜ × 8½. (Available in U.S. only) 25036-9 Pa. $4.95

VICTORIAN AND EDWARDIAN FASHION: A Photographic Survey, Alison Gernsheim. First fashion history completely illustrated by contemporary photographs. Full text plus 235 photos, 1840–1914, in which many celebrities appear. 240pp. 6½ × 9¼. 24205-6 Pa. $6.00

THE ART OF THE FRENCH ILLUSTRATED BOOK, 1700–1914, Gordon N. Ray. Over 630 superb book illustrations by Fragonard, Delacroix, Daumier, Doré, Grandville, Manet, Mucha, Steinlen, Toulouse-Lautrec and many others. Preface. Introduction. 633 halftones. Indices of artists, authors & titles, binders and provenances. Appendices. Bibliography. 608pp. 8⅜ × 11¼. 25086-5 Pa. $24.95

THE WONDERFUL WIZARD OF OZ, L. Frank Baum. Facsimile in full color of America's finest children's classic. 143 illustrations by W. W. Denslow. 267pp. 5⅜ × 8½. 20691-2 Pa. $5.95

FRONTIERS OF MODERN PHYSICS: New Perspectives on Cosmology, Relativity, Black Holes and Extraterrestrial Intelligence, Tony Rothman, et al. For the intelligent layman. Subjects include: cosmological models of the universe; black holes; the neutrino; the search for extraterrestrial intelligence. Introduction. 46 black-and-white illustrations. 192pp. 5⅜ × 8½. 24587-X Pa. $6.95

THE FRIENDLY STARS, Martha Evans Martin & Donald Howard Menzel. Classic text marshalls the stars together in an engaging, non-technical survey, presenting them as sources of beauty in night sky. 23 illustrations. Foreword. 2 star charts. Index. 147pp. 5⅜ × 8½. 21099-5 Pa. $3.50

FADS AND FALLACIES IN THE NAME OF SCIENCE, Martin Gardner. Fair, witty appraisal of cranks, quacks, and quackeries of science and pseudoscience: hollow earth, Velikovsky, orgone energy, Dianetics, flying saucers, Bridey Murphy, food and medical fads, etc. Revised, expanded In the Name of Science. "A very able and even-tempered presentation."—The New Yorker. 363pp. 5⅜ × 8. 20394-8 Pa. $5.95

ANCIENT EGYPT: ITS CULTURE AND HISTORY, J. E Manchip White. From pre-dynastics through Ptolemies: society, history, political structure, religion, daily life, literature, cultural heritage. 48 plates. 217pp. 5⅜ × 8½. 22548-8 Pa. $4.95

A CONCISE HISTORY OF PHOTOGRAPHY: Third Revised Edition, Helmut Gernsheim. Best one-volume history—camera obscura, photochemistry, daguerreotypes, evolution of cameras, film, more. Also artistic aspects—landscape, portraits, fine art, etc. 281 black-and-white photographs. 26 in color. 176pp. 8⅜ × 11¼. 25128-4 Pa. $12.95

THE DORÉ BIBLE ILLUSTRATIONS, Gustave Doré. 241 detailed plates from the Bible: the Creation scenes, Adam and Eve, Flood, Babylon, battle sequences, life of Jesus, etc. Each plate is accompanied by the verses from the King James version of the Bible. 241pp. 9 × 12. 23004-X Pa. $8.95

HUGGER-MUGGER IN THE LOUVRE, Elliot Paul. Second Homer Evans mystery-comedy. Theft at the Louvre involves sleuth in hilarious, madcap caper. "A knockout."—Books. 336pp. 5⅜ × 8½. 25185-3 Pa. $5.95

FLATLAND, E. A. Abbott. Intriguing and enormously popular science-fiction classic explores the complexities of trying to survive as a two-dimensional being in a three-dimensional world. Amusingly illustrated by the author. 16 illustrations. 103pp. 5⅜ × 8½. 20001-9 Pa. $2.00

THE HISTORY OF THE LEWIS AND CLARK EXPEDITION, Meriwether Lewis and William Clark, edited by Elliott Coues. Classic edition of Lewis and Clark's day-by-day journals that later became the basis for U.S. claims to Oregon and the West. Accurate and invaluable geographical, botanical, biological, meteorological and anthropological material. Total of 1,508pp. 5⅜ × 8½.
21268-8, 21269-6, 21270-X Pa. Three-vol. set $25.50

LANGUAGE, TRUTH AND LOGIC, Alfred J. Ayer. Famous, clear introduction to Vienna, Cambridge schools of Logical Positivism. Role of philosophy, elimination of metaphysics, nature of analysis, etc. 160pp. 5⅜ × 8½. (Available in U.S. and Canada only) 20010-8 Pa. $2.95

MATHEMATICS FOR THE NONMATHEMATICIAN, Morris Kline. Detailed, college-level treatment of mathematics in cultural and historical context, with numerous exercises. For liberal arts students. Preface. Recommended Reading Lists. Tables. Index. Numerous black-and-white figures. xvi + 641pp. 5⅜ × 8½.
24823-2 Pa. $11.95

28 SCIENCE FICTION STORIES, H. G. Wells. Novels, *Star Begotten* and *Men Like Gods,* plus 26 short stories: "Empire of the Ants," "A Story of the Stone Age," "The Stolen Bacillus," "In the Abyss," etc. 915pp. 5⅜ × 8½. (Available in U.S. only)
20265-8 Cloth. $10.95

HANDBOOK OF PICTORIAL SYMBOLS, Rudolph Modley. 3,250 signs and symbols, many systems in full; official or heavy commercial use. Arranged by subject. Most in Pictorial Archive series. 143pp. 8⅛ × 11. 23357-X Pa. $5.95

INCIDENTS OF TRAVEL IN YUCATAN, John L. Stephens. Classic (1843) exploration of jungles of Yucatan, looking for evidences of Maya civilization. Travel adventures, Mexican and Indian culture, etc. Total of 669pp. 5⅜ × 8½.
20926-1, 20927-X Pa., Two-vol. set $9.90

ILLUSTRATED GUIDE TO SHAKER FURNITURE, Robert Meader. All furniture and appurtenances, with much on unknown local styles. 235 photos. 146pp. 9 × 12. 22819-3 Pa. $7.95

WHALE SHIPS AND WHALING: A Pictorial Survey, George Francis Dow. Over 200 vintage engravings, drawings, photographs of barks, brigs, cutters, other vessels. Also harpoons, lances, whaling guns, many other artifacts. Comprehensive text by foremost authority. 207 black-and-white illustrations. 288pp. 6 × 9. 24808-9 Pa. $8.95

THE BERTRAMS, Anthony Trollope. Powerful portrayal of blind self-will and thwarted ambition includes one of Trollope's most heartrending love stories. 497pp. 5⅜ × 8½. 25119-5 Pa. $8.95

ADVENTURES WITH A HAND LENS, Richard Headstrom. Clearly written guide to observing and studying flowers and grasses, fish scales, moth and insect wings, egg cases, buds, feathers, seeds, leaf scars, moss, molds, ferns, common crystals, etc.—all with an ordinary, inexpensive magnifying glass. 209 exact line drawings aid in your discoveries. 220pp. 5⅜ × 8½. 23330-8 Pa. $3.95

RODIN ON ART AND ARTISTS, Auguste Rodin. Great sculptor's candid, wide-ranging comments on meaning of art; great artists; relation of sculpture to poetry, painting, music; philosophy of life, more. 76 superb black-and-white illustrations of Rodin's sculpture, drawings and prints. 119pp. 8⅜ × 11¼. 24487-3 Pa. $6.95

FIFTY CLASSIC FRENCH FILMS, 1912–1982: A Pictorial Record, Anthony Slide. Memorable stills from Grand Illusion, Beauty and the Beast, Hiroshima, Mon Amour, many more. Credits, plot synopses, reviews, etc. 160pp. 8¼ × 11. 25256-6 Pa. $11.95

THE PRINCIPLES OF PSYCHOLOGY, William James. Famous long course complete, unabridged. Stream of thought, time perception, memory, experimental methods; great work decades ahead of its time. 94 figures. 1,391pp. 5⅜ × 8½. 20381-6, 20382-4 Pa., Two-vol. set $19.90

BODIES IN A BOOKSHOP, R. T. Campbell. Challenging mystery of blackmail and murder with ingenious plot and superbly drawn characters. In the best tradition of British suspense fiction. 192pp. 5⅜ × 8½. 24720-1 Pa. $3.95

CALLAS: PORTRAIT OF A PRIMA DONNA, George Jellinek. Renowned commentator on the musical scene chronicles incredible career and life of the most controversial, fascinating, influential operatic personality of our time. 64 black-and-white photographs. 416pp. 5⅜ × 8¼. 25047-4 Pa. $7.95

GEOMETRY, RELATIVITY AND THE FOURTH DIMENSION, Rudolph Rucker. Exposition of fourth dimension, concepts of relativity as Flatland characters continue adventures. Popular, easily followed yet accurate, profound. 141 illustrations. 133pp. 5⅜ × 8½. 23400-2 Pa. $3.50

HOUSEHOLD STORIES BY THE BROTHERS GRIMM, with pictures by Walter Crane. 53 classic stories—Rumpelstiltskin, Rapunzel, Hansel and Gretel, the Fisherman and his Wife, Snow White, Tom Thumb, Sleeping Beauty, Cinderella, and so much more—lavishly illustrated with original 19th century drawings. 114 illustrations. x + 269pp. 5⅜ × 8½. 21080-4 Pa. $4.50

PLANTS OF THE BIBLE, Harold N. Moldenke and Alma L. Moldenke. Standard reference to all 230 plants mentioned in Scriptures. Latin name, biblical reference, uses, modern identity, much more. Unsurpassed encyclopedic resource for scholars, botanists, nature lovers, students of Bible. Bibliography. Indexes. 123 black-and-white illustrations. 384pp. 6 × 9. 25069-5 Pa. $8.95

FAMOUS AMERICAN WOMEN: A Biographical Dictionary from Colonial Times to the Present, Robert McHenry, ed. From Pocahontas to Rosa Parks, 1,035 distinguished American women documented in separate biographical entries. Accurate, up-to-date data, numerous categories, spans 400 years. Indices. 493pp. 6½ × 9¼. 24523-3 Pa. $9.95

THE FABULOUS INTERIORS OF THE GREAT OCEAN LINERS IN HISTORIC PHOTOGRAPHS, William H. Miller, Jr. Some 200 superb photographs capture exquisite interiors of world's great "floating palaces"—1890's to 1980's: *Titanic, Ile de France, Queen Elizabeth, United States, Europa*, more. Approx. 200 black-and-white photographs. Captions. Text. Introduction. 160pp. 8⅜ × 11¾. 24756-2 Pa. $9.95

THE GREAT LUXURY LINERS, 1927–1954: A Photographic Record, William H. Miller, Jr. Nostalgic tribute to heyday of ocean liners. 186 photos of Ile de France, Normandie, Leviathan, Queen Elizabeth, United States, many others. Interior and exterior views. Introduction. Captions. 160pp. 9 × 12. 24056-8 Pa. $9.95

A NATURAL HISTORY OF THE DUCKS, John Charles Phillips. Great landmark of ornithology offers complete detailed coverage of nearly 200 species and subspecies of ducks: gadwall, sheldrake, merganser, pintail, many more. 74 full-color plates, 102 black-and-white. Bibliography. Total of 1,920pp. 8⅜ × 11¼. 25141-1, 25142-X Cloth. Two-vol. set $100.00

THE SEAWEED HANDBOOK: An Illustrated Guide to Seaweeds from North Carolina to Canada, Thomas F. Lee. Concise reference covers 78 species. Scientific and common names, habitat, distribution, more. Finding keys for easy identification. 224pp. 5⅜ × 8½. 25215-9 Pa. $5.95

THE TEN BOOKS OF ARCHITECTURE: The 1755 Leoni Edition, Leon Battista Alberti. Rare classic helped introduce the glories of ancient architecture to the Renaissance. 68 black-and-white plates. 336pp. 8⅜ × 11¼. 25239-6 Pa. $14.95

MISS MACKENZIE, Anthony Trollope. Minor masterpieces by Victorian master unmasks many truths about life in 19th-century England. First inexpensive edition in years. 392pp. 5⅜ × 8½. 25201-9 Pa. $7.95

THE RIME OF THE ANCIENT MARINER, Gustave Doré, Samuel Taylor Coleridge. Dramatic engravings considered by many to be his greatest work. The terrifying space of the open sea, the storms and whirlpools of an unknown ocean, the ice of Antarctica, more—all rendered in a powerful, chilling manner. Full text. 38 plates. 77pp. 9¼ × 12. 22305-1 Pa. $4.95

THE EXPEDITIONS OF ZEBULON MONTGOMERY PIKE, Zebulon Montgomery Pike. Fascinating first-hand accounts (1805-6) of exploration of Mississippi River, Indian wars, capture by Spanish dragoons, much more. 1,088pp. 5⅜ × 8½. 25254-X, 25255-8 Pa. Two-vol. set $23.90

HOW TO WRITE, Gertrude Stein. Gertrude Stein claimed anyone could understand her unconventional writing—here are clues to help. Fascinating improvisations, language experiments, explanations illuminate Stein's craft and the art of writing. Total of 414pp. 4⅜ × 6⅜. 23144-5 Pa. $5.95

ADVENTURES AT SEA IN THE GREAT AGE OF SAIL: Five Firsthand Narratives, edited by Elliot Snow. Rare true accounts of exploration, whaling, shipwreck, fierce natives, trade, shipboard life, more. 33 illustrations. Introduction. 353pp. 5⅜ × 8½. 25177-2 Pa. $7.95

THE HERBAL OR GENERAL HISTORY OF PLANTS, John Gerard. Classic descriptions of about 2,850 plants—with over 2,700 illustrations—includes Latin and English names, physical descriptions, varieties, time and place of growth, more. 2,706 illustrations. xlv + 1,678pp. 8½ × 12¼. 23147-X Cloth. $75.00

DOROTHY AND THE WIZARD IN OZ, L. Frank Baum. Dorothy and the Wizard visit the center of the Earth, where people are vegetables, glass houses grow and Oz characters reappear. Classic sequel to *Wizard of Oz*. 256pp. 5⅜ × 8.
24714-7 Pa. $4.95

SONGS OF EXPERIENCE: Facsimile Reproduction with 26 Plates in Full Color, William Blake. This facsimile of Blake's original "Illuminated Book" reproduces 26 full-color plates from a rare 1826 edition. Includes "The Tyger," "London," "Holy Thursday," and other immortal poems. 26 color plates. Printed text of poems. 48pp. 5¼ × 7. 24636-1 Pa. $3.50

SONGS OF INNOCENCE, William Blake. The first and most popular of Blake's famous "Illuminated Books," in a facsimile edition reproducing all 31 brightly colored plates. Additional printed text of each poem. 64pp. 5¼ × 7.
22764-2 Pa. $3.50

PRECIOUS STONES, Max Bauer. Classic, thorough study of diamonds, rubies, emeralds, garnets, etc.: physical character, occurrence, properties, use, similar topics. 20 plates, 8 in color. 94 figures. 659pp. 6⅛ × 9¼.
21910-0, 21911-9 Pa., Two-vol. set $14.90

ENCYCLOPEDIA OF VICTORIAN NEEDLEWORK, S. F. A. Caulfeild and Blanche Saward. Full, precise descriptions of stitches, techniques for dozens of needlecrafts—most exhaustive reference of its kind. Over 800 figures. Total of 679pp. 8⅛ × 11. Two volumes. Vol. 1 22800-2 Pa. $10.95
Vol. 2 22801-0 Pa. $10.95

THE MARVELOUS LAND OF OZ, L. Frank Baum. Second Oz book, the Scarecrow and Tin Woodman are back with hero named Tip, Oz magic. 136 illustrations. 287pp. 5⅜ × 8½. 20692-0 Pa. $5.95

WILD FOWL DECOYS, Joel Barber. Basic book on the subject, by foremost authority and collector. Reveals history of decoy making and rigging, place in American culture, different kinds of decoys, how to make them, and how to use them. 140 plates. 156pp. 7⅞ × 10¾. 20011-6 Pa. $7.95

HISTORY OF LACE, Mrs. Bury Palliser. Definitive, profusely illustrated chronicle of lace from earliest times to late 19th century. Laces of Italy, Greece, England, France, Belgium, etc. Landmark of needlework scholarship. 266 illustrations. 672pp. 6⅛ × 9¼. 24742-2 Pa. $14.95

THE BLUE FAIRY BOOK, Andrew Lang. The first, most famous collection, with many familiar tales: Little Red Riding Hood, Aladdin and the Wonderful Lamp, Puss in Boots, Sleeping Beauty, Hansel and Gretel, Rumpelstiltskin; 37 in all. 138 illustrations. 390pp. 5⅜ × 8½.   21437-0 Pa. $5.95

THE STORY OF THE CHAMPIONS OF THE ROUND TABLE, Howard Pyle. Sir Launcelot, Sir Tristram and Sir Percival in spirited adventures of love and triumph retold in Pyle's inimitable style. 50 drawings, 31 full-page. xviii + 329pp. 6½ × 9¼.   21883-X Pa. $6.95

AUDUBON AND HIS JOURNALS, Maria Audubon. Unmatched two-volume portrait of the great artist, naturalist and author contains his journals, an excellent biography by his granddaughter, expert annotations by the noted ornithologist, Dr. Elliott Coues, and 37 superb illustrations. Total of 1,200pp. 5⅜ × 8.
Vol. I 25143-8 Pa. $8.95
Vol. II 25144-6 Pa. $8.95

GREAT DINOSAUR HUNTERS AND THEIR DISCOVERIES, Edwin H. Colbert. Fascinating, lavishly illustrated chronicle of dinosaur research, 1820's to 1960. Achievements of Cope, Marsh, Brown, Buckland, Mantell, Huxley, many others. 384pp. 5¼ × 8¼.   24701-5 Pa. $6.95

THE TASTEMAKERS, Russell Lynes. Informal, illustrated social history of American taste 1850's–1950's. First popularized categories Highbrow, Lowbrow, Middlebrow. 129 illustrations. New (1979) afterword. 384pp. 6 × 9.
23993-4 Pa. $6.95

DOUBLE CROSS PURPOSES, Ronald A. Knox. A treasure hunt in the Scottish Highlands, an old map, unidentified corpse, surprise discoveries keep reader guessing in this cleverly intricate tale of financial skullduggery. 2 black-and-white maps. 320pp. 5⅜ × 8½. (Available in U.S. only)   25032-6 Pa. $5.95

AUTHENTIC VICTORIAN DECORATION AND ORNAMENTATION IN FULL COLOR: 46 Plates from "Studies in Design," Christopher Dresser. Superb full-color lithographs reproduced from rare original portfolio of a major Victorian designer. 48pp. 9¼ × 12¼.   25083-0 Pa. $7.95

PRIMITIVE ART, Franz Boas. Remains the best text ever prepared on subject, thoroughly discussing Indian, African, Asian, Australian, and, especially, Northern American primitive art. Over 950 illustrations show ceramics, masks, totem poles, weapons, textiles, paintings, much more. 376pp. 5⅜ × 8. 20025-6 Pa. $6.95

SIDELIGHTS ON RELATIVITY, Albert Einstein. Unabridged republication of two lectures delivered by the great physicist in 1920–21. *Ether and Relativity* and *Geometry and Experience*. Elegant ideas in non-mathematical form, accessible to intelligent layman. vi + 56pp. 5⅜ × 8½.   24511-X Pa. $2.95

THE WIT AND HUMOR OF OSCAR WILDE, edited by Alvin Redman. More than 1,000 ripostes, paradoxes, wisecracks: Work is the curse of the drinking classes, I can resist everything except temptation, etc. 258pp. 5⅜ × 8½.   20602-5 Pa. $3.95

ADVENTURES WITH A MICROSCOPE, Richard Headstrom. 59 adventures with clothing fibers, protozoa, ferns and lichens, roots and leaves, much more. 142 illustrations. 232pp. 5⅜ × 8½.   23471-1 Pa. $3.95

CHRISTMAS CUSTOMS AND TRADITIONS, Clement A. Miles. Origin, evolution, significance of religious, secular practices. Caroling, gifts, yule logs, much more. Full, scholarly yet fascinating; non-sectarian. 400pp. 5⅜ × 8½.
23354-5 Pa. $6.50

THE HUMAN FIGURE IN MOTION, Eadweard Muybridge. More than 4,500 stopped-action photos, in action series, showing undraped men, women, children jumping, lying down, throwing, sitting, wrestling, carrying, etc. 390pp. 7⅞ × 10⅝.
20204-6 Cloth. $19.95

THE MAN WHO WAS THURSDAY, Gilbert Keith Chesterton. Witty, fast-paced novel about a club of anarchists in turn-of-the-century London. Brilliant social, religious, philosophical speculations. 128pp. 5⅜ × 8½. 25121-7 Pa. $3.95

A CEZANNE SKETCHBOOK: Figures, Portraits, Landscapes and Still Lifes, Paul Cezanne. Great artist experiments with tonal effects, light, mass, other qualities in over 100 drawings. A revealing view of developing master painter, precursor of Cubism. 102 black-and-white illustrations. 144pp. 8¾ × 6⅜. 24790-2 Pa. $5.95

AN ENCYCLOPEDIA OF BATTLES: Accounts of Over 1,560 Battles from 1479 B.C. to the Present, David Eggenberger. Presents essential details of every major battle in recorded history, from the first battle of Megiddo in 1479 B.C. to Grenada in 1984. List of Battle Maps. New Appendix covering the years 1967–1984. Index. 99 illustrations. 544pp. 6½ × 9¼. 24913-1 Pa. $14.95

AN ETYMOLOGICAL DICTIONARY OF MODERN ENGLISH, Ernest Weekley. Richest, fullest work, by foremost British lexicographer. Detailed word histories. Inexhaustible. Total of 856pp. 6½ × 9¼.
21873-2, 21874-0 Pa., Two-vol. set $17.00

WEBSTER'S AMERICAN MILITARY BIOGRAPHIES, edited by Robert McHenry. Over 1,000 figures who shaped 3 centuries of American military history. Detailed biographies of Nathan Hale, Douglas MacArthur, Mary Hallaren, others. Chronologies of engagements, more. Introduction. Addenda. 1,033 entries in alphabetical order. xi + 548pp. 6½ × 9¼. (Available in U.S. only)
24758-9 Pa. $11.95

LIFE IN ANCIENT EGYPT, Adolf Erman. Detailed older account, with much not in more recent books: domestic life, religion, magic, medicine, commerce, and whatever else needed for complete picture. Many illustrations. 597pp. 5⅜ × 8½.
22632-8 Pa. $8.50

HISTORIC COSTUME IN PICTURES, Braun & Schneider. Over 1,450 costumed figures shown, covering a wide variety of peoples: kings, emperors, nobles, priests, servants, soldiers, scholars, townsfolk, peasants, merchants, courtiers, cavaliers, and more. 256pp. 8⅜ × 11¼. 23150-X Pa. $7.95

THE NOTEBOOKS OF LEONARDO DA VINCI, edited by J. P. Richter. Extracts from manuscripts reveal great genius; on painting, sculpture, anatomy, sciences, geography, etc. Both Italian and English. 186 ms. pages reproduced, plus 500 additional drawings, including studies for *Last Supper, Sforza* monument, etc. 860pp. 7⅞ × 10¾. (Available in U.S. only) 22572-0, 22573-9 Pa., Two-vol. set $25.90

SUNDIALS, Albert Waugh. Far and away the best, most thorough coverage of ideas, mathematics concerned, types, construction, adjusting anywhere. Over 100 illustrations. 230pp. 5⅜ × 8½. 22947-5 Pa. $4.00

PICTURE HISTORY OF THE NORMANDIE: With 190 Illustrations, Frank O. Braynard. Full story of legendary French ocean liner: Art Deco interiors, design innovations, furnishings, celebrities, maiden voyage, tragic fire, much more. Extensive text. 144pp. 8⅞ × 11¾. 25257-4 Pa. $9.95

THE FIRST AMERICAN COOKBOOK: A Facsimile of "American Cookery," 1796, Amelia Simmons. Facsimile of the first American-written cookbook published in the United States contains authentic recipes for colonial favorites—pumpkin pudding, winter squash pudding, spruce beer, Indian slapjacks, and more. Introductory Essay and Glossary of colonial cooking terms. 80pp. 5⅜ × 8½. 24710-4 Pa. $3.50

101 PUZZLES IN THOUGHT AND LOGIC, C. R. Wylie, Jr. Solve murders and robberies, find out which fishermen are liars, how a blind man could possibly identify a color—purely by your own reasoning! 107pp. 5⅜ × 8½. 20367-0 Pa. $2.00

THE BOOK OF WORLD-FAMOUS MUSIC—CLASSICAL, POPULAR AND FOLK, James J. Fuld. Revised and enlarged republication of landmark work in musico-bibliography. Full information about nearly 1,000 songs and compositions including first lines of music and lyrics. New supplement. Index. 800pp. 5⅜ × 8¼. 24857-7 Pa. $14.95

ANTHROPOLOGY AND MODERN LIFE, Franz Boas. Great anthropologist's classic treatise on race and culture. Introduction by Ruth Bunzel. Only inexpensive paperback edition. 255pp. 5⅜ × 8½. 25245-0 Pa. $5.95

THE TALE OF PETER RABBIT, Beatrix Potter. The inimitable Peter's terrifying adventure in Mr. McGregor's garden, with all 27 wonderful, full-color Potter illustrations. 55pp. 4¼ × 5½. (Available in U.S. only) 22827-4 Pa. $1.75

THREE PROPHETIC SCIENCE FICTION NOVELS, H. G. Wells. *When the Sleeper Wakes, A Story of the Days to Come* and *The Time Machine* (full version). 335pp. 5⅜ × 8½. (Available in U.S. only) 20605-X Pa. $5.95

APICIUS COOKERY AND DINING IN IMPERIAL ROME, edited and translated by Joseph Dommers Vehling. Oldest known cookbook in existence offers readers a clear picture of what foods Romans ate, how they prepared them, etc. 49 illustrations. 301pp. 6⅛ × 9¼. 23563-7 Pa. $6.00

SHAKESPEARE LEXICON AND QUOTATION DICTIONARY, Alexander Schmidt. Full definitions, locations, shades of meaning of every word in plays and poems. More than 50,000 exact quotations. 1,485pp. 6½ × 9¼. 22726-X, 22727-8 Pa., Two-vol. set $27.90

THE WORLD'S GREAT SPEECHES, edited by Lewis Copeland and Lawrence W. Lamm. Vast collection of 278 speeches from Greeks to 1970. Powerful and effective models; unique look at history. 842pp. 5⅜ × 8½. 20468-5 Pa. $10.95

DEGAS: An Intimate Portrait, Ambroise Vollard. Charming, anecdotal memoir by famous art dealer of one of the greatest 19th-century French painters. 14 black-and-white illustrations. Introduction by Harold L. Van Doren. 96pp. 5⅜ × 8½.
25131-4 Pa. $3.95

PERSONAL NARRATIVE OF A PILGRIMAGE TO ALMANDINAH AND MECCAH, Richard Burton. Great travel classic by remarkably colorful personality. Burton, disguised as a Moroccan, visited sacred shrines of Islam, narrowly escaping death. 47 illustrations. 959pp. 5⅜ × 8½. 21217-3, 21218-1 Pa., Two-vol. set $17.90

PHRASE AND WORD ORIGINS, A. H. Holt. Entertaining, reliable, modern study of more than 1,200 colorful words, phrases, origins and histories. Much unexpected information. 254pp. 5⅜ × 8½. 20758-7 Pa. $4.95

THE RED THUMB MARK, R. Austin Freeman. In this first Dr. Thorndyke case, the great scientific detective draws fascinating conclusions from the nature of a single fingerprint. Exciting story, authentic science. 320pp. 5⅜ × 8½. (Available in U.S. only) 25210-8 Pa. $5.95

AN EGYPTIAN HIEROGLYPHIC DICTIONARY, E. A. Wallis Budge. Monumental work containing about 25,000 words or terms that occur in texts ranging from 3000 B.C. to 600 A.D. Each entry consists of a transliteration of the word, the word in hieroglyphs, and the meaning in English. 1,314pp. 6⅜ × 10.
23615-3, 23616-1 Pa., Two-vol. set $27.90

THE COMPLEAT STRATEGYST: Being a Primer on the Theory of Games of Strategy, J. D. Williams. Highly entertaining classic describes, with many illustrated examples, how to select best strategies in conflict situations. Prefaces. Appendices. xvi + 268pp. 5⅜ × 8½. 25101-2 Pa. $5.95

THE ROAD TO OZ, L. Frank Baum. Dorothy meets the Shaggy Man, little Button-Bright and the Rainbow's beautiful daughter in this delightful trip to the magical Land of Oz. 272pp. 5⅜ × 8. 25208-6 Pa. $4.95

POINT AND LINE TO PLANE, Wassily Kandinsky. Seminal exposition of role of point, line, other elements in non-objective painting. Essential to understanding 20th-century art. 127 illustrations. 192pp. 6½ × 9¼. 23808-3 Pa. $4.50

LADY ANNA, Anthony Trollope. Moving chronicle of Countess Lovel's bitter struggle to win for herself and daughter Anna their rightful rank and fortune—perhaps at cost of sanity itself. 384pp. 5⅜ × 8½. 24669-8 Pa. $6.95

EGYPTIAN MAGIC, E. A. Wallis Budge. Sums up all that is known about magic in Ancient Egypt: the role of magic in controlling the gods, powerful amulets that warded off evil spirits, scarabs of immortality, use of wax images, formulas and spells, the secret name, much more. 253pp. 5⅜ × 8½. 22681-6 Pa. $4.00

THE DANCE OF SIVA, Ananda Coomaraswamy. Preeminent authority unfolds the vast metaphysic of India: the revelation of her art, conception of the universe, social organization, etc. 27 reproductions of art masterpieces. 192pp. 5⅜ × 8½.
24817-8 Pa. $5.95

SIR HARRY HOTSPUR OF HUMBLETHWAITE, Anthony Trollope. Incisive, unconventional psychological study of a conflict between a wealthy baronet, his idealistic daughter, and their scapegrace cousin. The 1870 novel in its first inexpensive edition in years. 250pp. 5⅜ × 8½.   24953-0 Pa. $4.95

LASERS AND HOLOGRAPHY, Winston E. Kock. Sound introduction to burgeoning field, expanded (1981) for second edition. Wave patterns, coherence, lasers, diffraction, zone plates, properties of holograms, recent advances. 84 illustrations. 160pp. 5⅜ × 8¼. (Except in United Kingdom)   24041-X Pa. $3.50

INTRODUCTION TO ARTIFICIAL INTELLIGENCE: SECOND, EN-LARGED EDITION, Philip C. Jackson, Jr. Comprehensive survey of artificial intelligence—the study of how machines (computers) can be made to act intelligently. Includes introductory and advanced material. Extensive notes updating the main text. 132 black-and-white illustrations. 512pp. 5⅜ × 8½.   24864-X Pa. $8.95

HISTORY OF INDIAN AND INDONESIAN ART, Ananda K. Coomaraswamy. Over 400 illustrations illuminate classic study of Indian art from earliest Harappa finds to early 20th century. Provides philosophical, religious and social insights. 304pp. 6⅜ × 9⅜.   25005-9 Pa. $8.95

THE GOLEM, Gustav Meyrink. Most famous supernatural novel in modern European literature, set in Ghetto of Old Prague around 1890. Compelling story of mystical experiences, strange transformations, profound terror. 13 black-and-white illustrations. 224pp. 5⅜ × 8½. (Available in U.S. only)   25025-3 Pa. $5.95

ARMADALE, Wilkie Collins. Third great mystery novel by the author of *The Woman in White* and *The Moonstone*. Original magazine version with 40 illustrations. 597pp. 5⅜ × 8½.   23429-0 Pa. $7.95

PICTORIAL ENCYCLOPEDIA OF HISTORIC ARCHITECTURAL PLANS, DETAILS AND ELEMENTS: With 1,880 Line Drawings of Arches, Domes, Doorways, Facades, Gables, Windows, etc., John Theodore Haneman. Sourcebook of inspiration for architects, designers, others. Bibliography. Captions. 141pp. 9 × 12.   24605-1 Pa. $6.95

BENCHLEY LOST AND FOUND, Robert Benchley. Finest humor from early 30's, about pet peeves, child psychologists, post office and others. Mostly unavailable elsewhere. 73 illustrations by Peter Arno and others. 183pp. 5⅜ × 8½.
                   22410-4 Pa. $3.95

ERTÉ GRAPHICS, Erté. Collection of striking color graphics: *Seasons, Alphabet, Numerals, Aces* and *Precious Stones*. 50 plates, including 4 on covers. 48pp. 9⅜ × 12¼.   23580-7 Pa. $6.95

THE JOURNAL OF HENRY D. THOREAU, edited by Bradford Torrey, F. H. Allen. Complete reprinting of 14 volumes, 1837–61, over two million words; the sourcebooks for *Walden*, etc. Definitive. All original sketches, plus 75 photographs. 1,804pp. 8½ × 12¼.   20312-3, 20313-1 Cloth., Two-vol. set $80.00

CASTLES: THEIR CONSTRUCTION AND HISTORY, Sidney Toy. Traces castle development from ancient roots. Nearly 200 photographs and drawings illustrate moats, keeps, baileys, many other features. Caernarvon, Dover Castles, Hadrian's Wall, Tower of London, dozens more. 256pp. 5⅜ × 8¼.
                   24898-4 Pa. $5.95

ILLUSTRATED DICTIONARY OF HISTORIC ARCHITECTURE, edited by Cyril M. Harris. Extraordinary compendium of clear, concise definitions for over 5,000 important architectural terms complemented by over 2,000 line drawings. Covers full spectrum of architecture from ancient ruins to 20th-century Modernism. Preface. 592pp. 7½ × 9⅜. 24444-X Pa. $14.95

THE NIGHT BEFORE CHRISTMAS, Clement Moore. Full text, and woodcuts from original 1848 book. Also critical, historical material. 19 illustrations. 40pp. 4⅝ × 6. 22797-9 Pa. $2.25

THE LESSON OF JAPANESE ARCHITECTURE: 165 Photographs, Jiro Harada. Memorable gallery of 165 photographs taken in the 1930's of exquisite Japanese homes of the well-to-do and historic buildings. 13 line diagrams. 192pp. 8⅜ × 11¼. 24778-3 Pa. $8.95

THE AUTOBIOGRAPHY OF CHARLES DARWIN AND SELECTED LETTERS, edited by Francis Darwin. The fascinating life of eccentric genius composed of an intimate memoir by Darwin (intended for his children); commentary by his son, Francis; hundreds of fragments from notebooks, journals, papers; and letters to and from Lyell, Hooker, Huxley, Wallace and Henslow. xi + 365pp. 5⅜ × 8. 20479-0 Pa. $5.95

WONDERS OF THE SKY: Observing Rainbows, Comets, Eclipses, the Stars and Other Phenomena, Fred Schaaf. Charming, easy-to-read poetic guide to all manner of celestial events visible to the naked eye. Mock suns, glories, Belt of Venus, more. Illustrated. 299pp. 5¼ × 8¼. 24402-4 Pa. $7.95

BURNHAM'S CELESTIAL HANDBOOK, Robert Burnham, Jr. Thorough guide to the stars beyond our solar system. Exhaustive treatment. Alphabetical by constellation: Andromeda to Cetus in Vol. 1; Chamaeleon to Orion in Vol. 2; and Pavo to Vulpecula in Vol. 3. Hundreds of illustrations. Index in Vol. 3. 2,000pp. 6⅛ × 9¼. 23567-X, 23568-8, 23673-0 Pa., Three-vol. set $36.85

STAR NAMES: Their Lore and Meaning, Richard Hinckley Allen. Fascinating history of names various cultures have given to constellations and literary and folkloristic uses that have been made of stars. Indexes to subjects. Arabic and Greek names. Biblical references. Bibliography. 563pp. 5⅜ × 8½. 21079-0 Pa. $7.95

THIRTY YEARS THAT SHOOK PHYSICS: The Story of Quantum Theory, George Gamow. Lucid, accessible introduction to influential theory of energy and matter. Careful explanations of Dirac's anti-particles, Bohr's model of the atom, much more. 12 plates. Numerous drawings. 240pp. 5⅜ × 8½. 24895-X Pa. $4.95

CHINESE DOMESTIC FURNITURE IN PHOTOGRAPHS AND MEASURED DRAWINGS, Gustav Ecke. A rare volume, now affordably priced for antique collectors, furniture buffs and art historians. Detailed review of styles ranging from early Shang to late Ming. Unabridged republication. 161 black-and-white drawings, photos. Total of 224pp. 8⅜ × 11¼. (Available in U.S. only) 25171-3 Pa. $12.95

VINCENT VAN GOGH: A Biography, Julius Meier-Graefe. Dynamic, penetrating study of artist's life, relationship with brother, Theo, painting techniques, travels, more. Readable, engrossing. 160pp. 5⅜ × 8½. (Available in U.S. only) 25253-1 Pa. $3.95

AMERICAN CLIPPER SHIPS: 1833–1858, Octavius T. Howe & Frederick C. Matthews. Fully-illustrated, encyclopedic review of 352 clipper ships from the period of America's greatest maritime supremacy. Introduction. 109 halftones. 5 black-and-white line illustrations. Index. Total of 928pp. 5⅜ × 8½.
25115-2, 25116-0 Pa., Two-vol. set $17.90

TOWARDS A NEW ARCHITECTURE, Le Corbusier. Pioneering manifesto by great architect, near legendary founder of "International School." Technical and aesthetic theories, views on industry, economics, relation of form to function, "mass-production spirit," much more. Profusely illustrated. Unabridged translation of 13th French edition. Introduction by Frederick Etchells. 320pp. 6⅛ × 9¼. (Available in U.S. only)
25023-7 Pa. $8.95

THE BOOK OF KELLS, edited by Blanche Cirker. Inexpensive collection of 32 full-color, full-page plates from the greatest illuminated manuscript of the Middle Ages, painstakingly reproduced from rare facsimile edition. Publisher's Note. Captions. 32pp. 9⅜ × 12¼.
24345-1 Pa. $4.50

BEST SCIENCE FICTION STORIES OF H. G. WELLS, H. G. Wells. Full novel *The Invisible Man*, plus 17 short stories: "The Crystal Egg," "Aepyornis Island," "The Strange Orchid," etc. 303pp. 5⅜ × 8½. (Available in U.S. only)
21531-8 Pa. $4.95

AMERICAN SAILING SHIPS: Their Plans and History, Charles G. Davis. Photos, construction details of schooners, frigates, clippers, other sailcraft of 18th to early 20th centuries—plus entertaining discourse on design, rigging, nautical lore, much more. 137 black-and-white illustrations. 240pp. 6⅛ × 9¼.
24658-2 Pa. $5.95

ENTERTAINING MATHEMATICAL PUZZLES, Martin Gardner. Selection of author's favorite conundrums involving arithmetic, money, speed, etc., with lively commentary. Complete solutions. 112pp. 5⅜ × 8½.   25211-6 Pa. $2.95

THE WILL TO BELIEVE, HUMAN IMMORTALITY, William James. Two books bound together. Effect of irrational on logical, and arguments for human immortality. 402pp. 5⅜ × 8½.   20291-7 Pa. $7.50

THE HAUNTED MONASTERY and THE CHINESE MAZE MURDERS, Robert Van Gulik. 2 full novels by Van Gulik continue adventures of Judge Dee and his companions. An evil Taoist monastery, seemingly supernatural events; overgrown topiary maze that hides strange crimes. Set in 7th-century China. 27 illustrations. 328pp. 5⅜ × 8½.   23502-5 Pa. $5.00

CELEBRATED CASES OF JUDGE DEE (DEE GOONG AN), translated by Robert Van Gulik. Authentic 18th-century Chinese detective novel; Dee and associates solve three interlocked cases. Led to Van Gulik's own stories with same characters. Extensive introduction. 9 illustrations. 237pp. 5⅜ × 8½.
23337-5 Pa. $4.95